Better Homes and Gardens®

E A T I N G
LIGHT

© Copyright 1985 by Meredith Corporation, Des Moines, Iowa.
All Rights Reserved. Printed in the United States of America.
First Edition. Seventh Printing, 1989.
Library of Congress Catalog Card Number: 84-61308
ISBN: 0-696-01475-0

BETTER HOMES AND GARDENS® BOOKS
Editor: Gerald M. Knox
Art Director: Ernest Shelton
Managing Editor: David A. Kirchner

Food and Nutrition Editor: Nancy Byal
Department Head—Cook Books: Sharyl Heiken
Associate Department Heads: Sandra Granseth,
    Rosemary C. Hutchinson, Elizabeth Woolever
Senior Food Editors: Julia Malloy, Marcia Stanley,
    Joyce Trollope
Associate Food Editors: Barbara Atkins, Molly Culbertson,
    Linda Foley, Linda Henry, Lynn Hoppe, Jill Johnson,
    Mary Jo Plutt, Maureen Powers
Recipe Development Editor: Marion Viall
Test Kitchen Director: Sharon Stilwell
Test Kitchen Photo Studio Director: Janet Pittman
Test Kitchen Home Economists: Jean Brekke, Kay Cargill,
    Marilyn Cornelius, Maryellyn Krantz, Lynelle Munn,
    Dianna Nolin, Marge Steenson, Cynthia Volcko

Associate Art Directors: Linda Ford Vermie,
    Neoma Alt West, Randall Yontz
Copy and Production Editors: Marsha Jahns,
    Mary Helen Schiltz, Carl Voss, David A. Walsh
Assistant Art Directors: Faith Berven, Harijs Priekulis,
    Tom Wegner
Senior Graphic Designers: Alisann Dixon, Lynda Haupert,
    Lyne Neymeyer
Graphic Designers: Mike Burns, Mike Eagleton, Deb Miner,
    Stan Sams, D. Greg Thompson, Darla Whipple-Frain

Vice President, Editorial Director: Doris Eby
Executive Director, Editorial Services: Duane L. Gregg

General Manager: Fred Stines
Director of Publishing: Robert B. Nelson
Vice President, Retail Marketing: Jamie Martin
Vice President, Direct Marketing: Arthur Heydendael

EATING LIGHT
Editor: Linda Henry
Copy and Production Editor: Carl Voss
Graphic Designers: D. Greg Thompson, Randall Yontz
Contributing Photographers: M. Jensen Photography, Inc.,
    Scott Little
Food Stylists: Janet Pittman, Bonnie Rabert
Electronic Text Processor: Joyce Wasson

On the cover: *Ham and Fruit Toss (see recipe, page 45)*

Our seal assures you that every recipe in *Eating Light* has been tested in the Better Homes and Gardens® Test Kitchen. This means that each recipe is practical and reliable, and meets our high standards of taste appeal.

There's an inclination in today's world toward lighter, fresher, and simpler meals. *Eating Light* will introduce you to this new direction and help you fit it into *your* life-style.

Eating Light is packed with intriguing new recipes that blend enticing flavors and textures, and play up fresh-tasting ingredients. We carefully selected all the ingredients and seasonings so they heighten instead of mask the natural goodness of the food. Herbs and spices accent the food in many of the recipes; citrus fruits, which seem to be naturals when you're looking for a light and refreshing taste, step up the flavor in other recipes.

Throughout the book, the foods are broiled, steamed, poached, and stir-fried—methods of cooking that enhance lean meat, poultry, and fish, and enable you to feel good about what you eat.

All in all, these recipes create nutritious and satisfying dishes that add variety and irresistible flavor to your newfound "light" life-style.

Savory Lean Meats

The lean cuts of beef, pork, and lamb featured in this chapter adapt to both hearty, home-style dishes and to glamorous entrées. The variety of full-flavored eating possibilities adds up to a number of satisfying dishes.

Grilled Steak with Italian Vegetables

A pepper mill makes quick work out of cracking whole black pepper. But if you need a backup method, press the pepper against the side of a small bowl with the back of a metal spoon.

1   1-pound beef top loin steak, cut 1 inch thick
1   teaspoon whole black pepper
1   tablespoon butter *or* margarine
4   green onions, bias sliced into 1-inch pieces
3   medium zucchini, cut into julienne strips
1   small green pepper, cut into strips
1   clove garlic, minced
½   teaspoon dried oregano, crushed, *or* 1½ teaspoons snipped fresh oregano
12 cherry tomatoes, halved

● Trim steak of excess fat. Coarsely crack the whole black pepper; sprinkle meat with *half* of the cracked pepper. Rub pepper over meat and press in with heel of hand. Turn steak and repeat with remaining cracked pepper.

● Grill steak over *medium-hot* coals to desired doneness, turning once (allow 15 to 16 minutes total time for rare; 18 to 20 minutes for medium). Or, broil 3 inches from heat to desired doneness, turning once (allow 8 to 10 minutes total time for rare; 12 to 14 minutes for medium).

● Meanwhile, melt butter or margarine. Add sliced green onions, zucchini strips, green pepper strips, garlic, and oregano. Cook and stir for 4 minutes; stir in cherry tomato halves. Cover and cook for 1 minute more.

● To serve, slice meat diagonally across the grain. Serve steak with cooked vegetables. Makes 4 servings.

Stuffed Flank Steak Teriyaki

Friends coming for dinner? Impress them with your cooking talents by featuring this handsome marinated entrée.

1   1¼-pound beef flank steak
½   cup soy sauce
¼   cup cooking oil
2   tablespoons molasses
2   teaspoons dry mustard
1   teaspoon grated gingerroot
1   clove garlic, minced
1   cup water
1   medium carrot, shredded (½ cup)
½   cup long grain rice
½   cup sliced water chestnuts
¼   cup sliced green onion

● To cut a pocket in flank steak, insert the tip of a long-bladed knife horizontally into the short end of the steak. Slit a pocket the full width and length of the steak, cutting to, but not through edges, so steak remains connected on three sides.

● For marinade, combine soy sauce, cooking oil, molasses, dry mustard, gingerroot, and garlic. Place meat in a clear plastic bag; set in a bowl. Pour marinade into pocket and over meat. Close bag. Let stand at room temperature about 30 minutes, turning bag occasionally.

● For stuffing, in a small saucepan combine water, shredded carrot, rice, water chestnuts, and green onion. Bring to boiling; reduce heat. Cover and simmer about 8 minutes or till rice is done. Remove from heat.

● Remove meat from marinade; reserve marinade. Stir ¼ *cup* of the reserved marinade into stuffing. Spoon stuffing into pocket cut in meat. Secure with small skewers or wooden toothpicks. Place meat in a shallow roasting pan; cover with foil.

● Bake in a 350° oven about 1 hour or till meat is done, brushing occasionally with the reserved marinade. To serve, slice meat diagonally across the grain; brush with marinade just before serving. Makes 6 servings.

Pork Pinwheels with
Apricot Stuffing
(see recipe, page 13)

Oriental Beef and Vegetable Stir-Fry

Flavorful bok choy adds a rich green color to stir-fry dishes.

¾ pound beef top round steak
2 teaspoons cornstarch
1 teaspoon sugar
¼ teaspoon instant beef
   bouillon granules
¼ cup dry sherry
¼ cup water
3 tablespoons soy sauce
2 tablespoons cooking oil
2 tablespoons sliced green
   onion
1 clove garlic, minced
1 teaspoon grated gingerroot
1 8-ounce can sliced water
   chestnuts, drained
1 6-ounce package frozen pea
   pods, thawed, *or* 1 cup
   fresh pea pods
2 cups chopped bok choy
   Hot cooked rice

● Partially freeze beef; cut on the bias into bite-size strips. Set beef aside.

● Stir together cornstarch, sugar, and beef bouillon granules. Stir in sherry, water, and soy sauce. Set aside.

● Preheat a wok or large skillet over high heat; add *1 table-spoon* cooking oil. Stir-fry the green onion, garlic, and ginger-root for 30 seconds. Add the drained water chestnuts and pea pods. Stir-fry for 1 to 2 minutes or till pea pods are crisp-tender. Remove vegetables from the wok or skillet.

● Add the remaining oil to the wok or skillet. Add *half* of the meat to the wok or skillet. Stir-fry about 2 minutes or till done. Remove the meat. Stir-fry the remaining meat about 2 minutes or till done. Return all the meat to the wok or skillet.

● Stir the sherry mixture; stir into meat. Cook and stir till thickened and bubbly. Cook and stir for 30 seconds more. Stir in cooked vegetables and bok choy. Cover and cook about 1 minute more or till heated through. Serve over hot cooked rice. Makes 4 servings.

Stir-frying vegetables
Once you start to stir-fry, it's best not to stop. That's why you'll want to prepare all the ingredients in advance, and put them within easy reach of your wok.

As you begin stir-frying, pour the cooking oil in a ring around the upper part of the preheated wok so it coats the sides as it runs to the center.

Add the green onion, garlic, and gingerroot; stir-fry for 30 seconds. Use a long-handled spatula or spoon to stir-fry. Gently lift and turn the food with a folding motion. Next, stir-fry water chestnuts and pea pods for 1 to 2 minutes, as shown.

Keep the food moving at all times, or it will burn quickly.

Broiled Vegetable Burgers

Use the tangy Tomato-Cucumber Relish to liven up any burger.

1 pound lean ground beef
1 medium carrot, shredded
    (½ cup)
¼ cup finely chopped green
    pepper
¼ cup finely chopped onion
½ teaspoon seasoned salt
    Dash pepper
2 cups fresh alfalfa sprouts
¼ cup Tomato-Cucumber
    Relish

● Combine ground beef, shredded carrot, chopped green pepper, chopped onion, seasoned salt, and pepper. Shape mixture into four ½-inch-thick patties.

● Place patties on rack of an unheated broiler pan. Broil 3 inches from heat to desired doneness, turning once (allow about 8 minutes total time for rare; about 10 minutes for medium; about 12 minutes for well-done).

● Place each broiled patty on a bed of fresh alfalfa sprouts. Spoon *1 tablespoon* of the Tomato-Cucumber Relish atop each patty. Makes 4 servings.

Tomato-Cucumber Relish: Combine ¼ cup *vinegar*, ¼ cup *water*, 2 tablespoons *sugar*, ½ teaspoon *salt*, and ⅛ teaspoon *pepper*. Stir in 1 medium *tomato*, chopped (1 cup); ½ of a small *cucumber*, chopped (⅔ cup); and 1 medium *onion*, chopped (½ cup). Cover and refrigerate for 1 to 2 hours. Before serving, drain well; stir in ¼ cup chopped *dill pickle*. Keep the unused Tomato-Cucumber Relish tightly covered in the refrigerator for up to 5 days. Makes 2 cups relish.

Ground Beef Facts

Federal and state laws regulate ground beef content. It cannot be less than 70% lean or contain other meats or cereals.

Most ground beef products are labeled according to meat industry recommendations. The quality distinction between types of ground beef is indicated on the label by the phrase, "Not less than X% lean." Often, it is labeled as ground chuck, ground round, or ground sirloin to indicate that all the meat is from a specific cut. Ground round is the most lean, followed by ground sirloin, and ground chuck.

Consider buying ground chuck if you plan to broil the ground beef (as you might for burgers), or if you need to break up, cook, and drain it (as you would for a casserole). It costs less, and although it contains more fat to begin with, the fat content of cooked ground chuck is about the same as leaner ground beef after cooking.

Fruit and Lamb Kabobs

Fruit and Lamb Kabobs

When they're in season, try substituting fresh plums, pitted and quartered, for the apple wedges.

¼ cup frozen apple juice
  concentrate
1 tablespoon lemon juice
1 teaspoon Worcestershire
  sauce
¼ teaspoon ground cinnamon
¼ teaspoon ground ginger
1 pound boneless lamb, cut
  into 1-inch pieces
1 papaya, peeled, halved, and
  seeded
2 *or* 3 medium apples, cored
  and cut into wedges
  Hot cooked couscous *or*
  bulgur (optional)

● For marinade, combine apple juice concentrate, lemon juice, Worcestershire sauce, cinnamon, and ginger. Place the lamb pieces in a plastic bag; set the bag in a bowl. Pour the marinade over the lamb. Close bag; turn to evenly distribute marinade. Let the lamb stand several hours or overnight in the refrigerator, turning occasionally.

● Drain lamb, reserving marinade. Cut the papaya into 1- to 1½-inch pieces. On 5 skewers alternately thread lamb pieces, papaya pieces, and apples wedges.

● Place skewers on the rack of an unheated broiler pan. Broil 4 inches from heat for 12 to 15 minutes or till lamb is done, turning occasionally and brushing with reserved marinade.

● Serve the kabobs with hot cooked couscous or bulgur, if desired. Makes 5 servings.

Hints for Cooking Light

Steaming, poaching, broiling, and stir-frying—undoubtedly you already know something about these four ways of cooking. But what you may not realize is that they are right in step with eating light.

Steaming has always been a popular way to cook vegetables, but it's just as suitable for meat, fish, and chicken. The process is simple—food is suspended over boiling water so the steam from the water does the cooking. Foods retain their natural freshness, flavor, and texture.

Poaching is simply simmering foods in a moderate amount of liquid.

It requires no fat, and the cooking liquid becomes an ideal base for a sauce.

Broiling holds natural flavor and juices inside foods. Because food is cooked on a rack by very hot direct heat, many of the fats present in foods are left behind in the broiler pan.

Stir-fry dishes combine a small amount of meat with a generous selection of vegetables, all cooked in a minimum amount of oil. The brief cooking time helps foods retain their texture, color, and flavor.

Lemony Lamb Chops

Just a hint of oregano rounds out the flavor of the tangy lemon sauce.

2 teaspoons cornstarch
¼ teaspoon salt
⅛ teaspoon dried oregano, crushed
  Dash pepper
½ cup water
1 teaspoon Worcestershire sauce
¼ teaspoon finely shredded lemon peel
2 tablespoons lemon juice
4 lamb loin chops, cut ¾ inch thick (about 1¼ pounds total)

● For lemon sauce, combine cornstarch, salt, oregano, and pepper; stir in water and Worcestershire sauce. Cook and stir till thickened and bubbly; cook and stir 2 minutes more. Stir in lemon peel and lemon juice.
● Trim chops of excess fat. Place chops on the rack of an unheated broiler pan; brush chops with some of the lemon sauce.
● Broil 3 to 4 inches from heat to desired doneness, turning and brushing with sauce once (allow 10 to 12 minutes total time for medium; 14 to 16 minutes for well-done). Pass remaining lemon sauce with chops. Makes 4 servings.

Measuring the distance from the broiler heat source
Trim the excess fat off the lamb chops. Place the chops on the rack of an unheated broiler pan. (If you don't have a broiler pan, improvise by placing a wire rack in a shallow baking pan.)

Use a ruler to measure the distance from the top of the meat to the heat source, as shown. If you need to, adjust the oven rack so the meat is the correct distance from the heat.

Broil the meat to the desired doneness according to the recipe directions.

Pork Pinwheels with Apricot Stuffing

The most tender of all pork cuts, pork tenderloin makes a great impression on dinner guests. (Pictured on page 7.)

1   1-pound pork tenderloin
1   teaspoon instant chicken
    bouillon granules
⅔   cup hot water
⅓   cup snipped dried apricots
2   tablespoons chopped onion
2   tablespoons chopped celery
1   tablespoon butter *or*
    margarine
⅛   teaspoon ground cinnamon
    Dash pepper
2   cups dry whole wheat bread
    cubes
1½ teaspoons cornstarch
    Dash ground nutmeg
1   cup apricot nectar

● Split tenderloin lengthwise, cutting to, but not through, opposite side; open out flat. Working out from center, pound tenderloin lightly with meat mallet to about a 10x6-inch rectangle.
● For stuffing, dissolve bouillon in hot water; pour over apricots. Let stand 5 minutes. Cook onion and celery in butter or margarine till tender but not brown. Remove from heat; stir in cinnamon and pepper. Place the dry bread cubes in a large mixing bowl. Add the onion mixture and the apricot mixture; toss lightly to moisten.
● Spread stuffing evenly over tenderloin. Roll up jelly-roll style, starting from one of the short sides. Secure meat roll with wooden toothpicks or tie with string at 1-inch intervals. Cut meat roll into six 1-inch slices.
● Place meat slices on rack of unheated broiler pan, cut side down. Broil 4 inches from heat for 12 minutes. Turn; broil for 11 to 13 minutes more or till done. Remove toothpicks or string; transfer meat to a serving platter.
● Meanwhile, for sauce, combine cornstarch and ground nutmeg. Stir in apricot nectar. Cook and stir till mixture is thickened and bubbly. Cook and stir 2 minutes more. Serve sauce with meat slices. Makes 6 servings.

Broiled Pork Chops and Vegetables

You can cook this entire meal under your broiler.

3   tablespoons cooking oil
3   tablespoons dry red wine
1   tablespoon finely chopped
    green onion
1   tablespoon honey
¾   teaspoon dried oregano,
    crushed
¾   teaspoon dried basil,
    crushed
⅛   teaspoon garlic powder
    Dash pepper
4   pork loin chops, cut 1 to 1¼
    inches thick (about 1¾
    pounds total)
12 large whole fresh
    mushrooms
2   medium tomatoes, halved
2   tablespoons grated
    Parmesan cheese

● Combine oil, red wine, green onion, honey, oregano, basil, garlic powder, and pepper; set aside.
● Trim chops of excess fat. Place chops on the rack of an unheated broiler pan. Broil chops 3 to 4 inches from heat about 12 minutes; brush with wine mixture. Turn chops. Arrange mushrooms and tomato halves on broiling rack around the chops.
● Continue broiling for 10 to 12 minutes more or till chops are almost done, brushing chops and mushrooms with wine mixture. Sprinkle Parmesan cheese atop tomatoes. Broil about 2 minutes more.
● Place chops on a platter; surround with mushrooms and tomato halves. Makes 4 servings.

Sweet and Sour Pork

Typically in sweet and sour pork recipes, the meat is coated with a batter and deep-fat fried. Our lighter version eliminates this high-calorie cooking method.

1 8-ounce can pineapple
   chunks (juice pack)
1 pound lean boneless pork
2 tablespoons cornstarch
1 cup chicken broth
¼ cup red wine vinegar
2 tablespoons brown sugar
2 teaspoons soy sauce
1 tablespoon cooking oil
1 clove garlic, minced
1 large green pepper, cut
   into 1-inch pieces
1 medium carrot, very thinly
   bias sliced
   Chow mein noodles

● Drain pineapple chunks, reserving ⅓ cup juice. Set pineapple chunks and juice aside. Cut pork into ½-inch cubes. Set aside.

● Combine reserved pineapple juice and cornstarch; stir in chicken broth, red wine vinegar, brown sugar, and soy sauce; set aside.

● Preheat a wok or large skillet over high heat; add oil. Stir-fry the garlic, green pepper, and carrot in the hot oil about 2 minutes or till vegetables are crisp-tender. Remove the vegetables from the wok.

● Add *half* of the pork cubes to the wok. Stir-fry for 2 to 3 minutes or till no longer pink. Remove pork. Stir-fry remaining pork for 2 to 3 minutes or till no longer pink. Return all pork to wok or skillet.

● Stir pineapple juice mixture; stir into wok. Cook and stir till mixture is thickened and bubbly. Cook and stir for 2 minutes more. Stir in the drained pineapple chunks and the vegetables. Cover and cook about 2 minutes more or till heated through. Serve over chow mein noodles. Makes 6 servings.

Veal Loaf

When chilled and sliced, this loaf becomes the lunchtime answer for a hungry sandwich lover.

2 eggs
¾ cup milk
½ cup fine dry bread crumbs
½ cup shredded carrot
¼ cup finely chopped onion
2 tablespoons snipped parsley
1 teaspoon salt
   Dash pepper
1½ pounds ground veal

● Combine eggs and milk; stir in bread crumbs, shredded carrot, chopped onion, snipped parsley, salt, and pepper. Add the ground veal; mix well.

● Pat veal mixture into an 8x4x2-inch loaf pan. Bake in a 350° oven about 1½ hours. Drain off excess fat. Let loaf stand for 15 minutes before turning out of pan. Makes 6 servings.

Poultry, Fish, and Seafood

These versatile foods provide
many delectable and imaginative
entrées guaranteed to please.
From Herbed Chicken à la
Française to Easy Oven-Fried
Fish, the broad range of recipes
will delight sophisticated
diners as well as those whose
preference is toward
simpler cooking.

Citrus-Glazed Chicken

If you can't get the chicken far enough away from the heat, remove the broiler rack and broil the chicken in the bottom of the broiler pan.

1 8-ounce can pineapple slices (juice pack)
2 tablespoons butter *or* margarine
1 teaspoon finely shredded lemon peel
1 tablespoon lemon juice
1 2½- to 3-pound broiler-fryer chicken, cut up
   Orange slices (optional)
   Watercress (optional)

● Drain the pineapple slices, reserving 2 tablespoons juice; set pineapple slices and juice aside.
● For citrus glaze, melt butter or margarine. Stir in reserved pineapple juice, lemon peel, and lemon juice; set aside.
● Place the chicken pieces, skin side down, on the rack of an unheated broiler pan. Place under broiler unit with surface of chicken 5 to 6 inches from heat. Broil about 20 minutes or till lightly browned. Brush chicken pieces with citrus glaze.
● Turn chicken pieces skin side up and broil for 15 to 20 minutes more or till tender, brushing occasionally with glaze. Add pineapple slices to broiler rack the last 5 minutes of broiling.
● Remove the chicken pieces and pineapple slices from the broiler rack. Garnish with orange slices and watercress, if desired. Makes 6 servings.

Hidden Salt

Most of us consume much more salt than we really need. Sometimes people salt food even before tasting it—more out of habit than because the food really needs it!

To begin cutting back on your salt intake, you need to remove the salt shaker from your table, *and* become aware of where sodium, a major component of salt, hides in the foods you eat each day.

Canned soups are high in salt, as are canned meats such as tuna and chicken. Canned vegetables contain higher amounts of salt than do frozen vegetables.

Condiments such as catsup, mustard, and mayonnaise are high in salt, and pickles and olives are very salty. Snack items such as potato chips, popcorn, and peanuts can be extremely high in salt.

Many manufacturers have introduced procedures that lower salt in their products. Watch for these specially marked products in your supermarket. If you can begin to limit your use of high-sodium foods, you've taken a big step forward in controlling your salt consumption.

Citrus-Glazed Chicken

Mexicali Oven-Fried Chicken

Do you count calories? If so, you can save about 20 calories per serving just by removing the skin from the chicken.

⅓ cup yellow cornmeal
1 tablespoon all-purpose flour
1 teaspoon dried oregano, crushed
1 teaspoon chili powder
1 2½- to 3-pound broiler-fryer chicken, cut up
2 tablespoons butter *or* margarine, melted

● In a bowl combine the cornmeal, flour, dried oregano, and chili powder; place cornmeal mixture on a sheet of waxed paper. Set aside.
● To skin the chicken pieces, use your fingers to pull the skin away from the meat; discard the skin (see photograph, page 20). Rinse the chicken pieces. Roll the chicken pieces in the cornmeal mixture to coat evenly.
● Arrange the coated chicken pieces in an ungreased 15x10x1-inch baking pan. Pour the melted butter or margarine evenly over the chicken pieces.
● Bake chicken in a 375° oven about 50 minutes or till tender. *Do not turn.* (Chicken is done when it is easily pierced with a fork. Test the thigh or breast at a point near the bone, since these parts require the most cooking time.) Makes 6 servings.

Chicken Florentine

"Florentine" is a recipe term that's used when spinach is an ingredient. The entrée usually is served on a bed of cooked spinach, with a sauce spooned over the top.

2 medium chicken breasts, halved lengthwise
⅛ teaspoon pepper
¾ cup chicken broth
2 tablespoons dry white wine
1 pound spinach
1 tablespoon cold water
2 teaspoons cornstarch
3 ounces Neufchâtel cheese, cut up
   Lemon juice
   Paprika
   Lemon slices (optional)

● Skin and bone chicken breast halves (see photographs, pages 20 and 21). Place chicken breasts in a skillet; sprinkle with pepper. Combine chicken broth and white wine; add to skillet. Bring to boiling. Reduce heat; cover and simmer for 25 to 30 minutes or till chicken is tender.
● Meanwhile, rinse the spinach in cool water. In a saucepan cook spinach, covered, in just the water that clings to the spinach leaves. Reduce heat when steam forms. Continue cooking spinach for 3 to 5 minutes after steam forms, turning frequently with a fork. Set spinach aside.
● Remove chicken breasts from skillet with a slotted spoon, reserving the broth mixture. Keep chicken warm.
● To make sauce, combine the 1 tablespoon water and cornstarch; stir into broth mixture in skillet. Cook and stir till thickened and bubbly. Cook and stir 2 minutes more. Add cut-up Neufchâtel cheese, stirring till cheese is melted.
● Arrange cooked spinach on a serving platter; sprinkle with lemon juice. Place chicken breasts atop spinach; pour sauce over all. Sprinkle with paprika. Garnish with lemon slices, if desired. Makes 4 servings.

Chicken Pineapple Dijon

Herbs, spices, and white wine give French-style Dijon mustard its special flavor.

3 medium chicken breasts,
   halved lengthwise
 Salt
 Pepper
 Paprika
1 8¼-ounce can crushed
   pineapple (juice pack)
2 tablespoons cold water
1 tablespoon Dijon-style
   mustard
1 teaspoon cornstarch

● Skin and bone chicken breast halves (see photographs, pages 20 and 21). Place each chicken breast half between two pieces of clear plastic wrap. Use a meat mallet to pound each piece of chicken slightly. Season each piece of chicken with salt, pepper, and paprika.

● Arrange chicken pieces in an ungreased 12x7½x2-inch baking dish. Cover and bake in a 375° oven about 25 minutes or till tender. Drain juices from pan.

● Meanwhile, for sauce, combine *undrained* crushed pineapple, water, mustard, and cornstarch. Cook and stir till thickened and bubbly. Cook and stir 2 minutes more. Spoon sauce over drained chicken pieces. Return chicken to oven; bake about 5 minutes more. Makes 6 servings.

Orange-Glazed Chicken

Here's a tip to keep unused gingerroot fresh: For short-term storage, keep it wrapped in the refrigerator. For longer storage, freeze the unpeeled gingerroot; cut off what you need while it's frozen.

2 medium chicken breasts,
   halved lengthwise
½ teaspoon finely shredded
   orange peel
3 tablespoons orange juice
2 tablespoons soy sauce
2 teaspoons cornstarch
1 teaspoon grated gingerroot
2 tablespoons cooking oil
6 green onions, bias sliced
   into 1-inch lengths
1 cup sliced fresh mushrooms
½ of a 10-ounce package
   frozen peas, thawed

● Skin and bone chicken breast halves (see photographs, pages 20 and 21). Cut chicken into 1-inch pieces. Set aside.

● Stir together orange peel, orange juice, soy sauce, cornstarch, and gingerroot. Set aside.

● Preheat a wok or large skillet over high heat; add *1 tablespoon* cooking oil. Stir-fry green onions about 2 minutes or till crisp-tender. Remove green onions from wok or skillet. Add the sliced mushrooms and thawed peas; stir-fry for 2 minutes. Remove from wok or skillet.

● Add the remaining oil to the wok or skillet. Add *half* of the chicken to the wok or skillet. Stir-fry for 2 minutes or till done. Remove the chicken. Stir-fry remaining chicken for 2 minutes or till done. Return all chicken to wok or skillet.

● Stir orange juice mixture; stir into chicken. Cook and stir till thickened and bubbly. Cook and stir for 30 seconds more. Stir in onions, mushrooms, and peas. Cook and stir about 1 minute more or till heated through. Makes 4 servings.

Herbed Chicken à la Francaise

Tarragon, an aromatic herb, has a hint of licorice flavor.

2 medium chicken breasts,
   halved lengthwise
2 green onions, sliced
½ teaspoon dried tarragon,
   crushed
1 tablespoon butter *or*
   margarine
   Salt
   Pepper
⅓ cup dry white wine *or*
   chicken broth
1 egg white
½ cup mayonnaise *or*
   salad dressing
1 tablespoon grated
   Parmesan cheese
1 tablespoon snipped parsley

● Skin and bone chicken breast halves (see photographs, below and opposite). Arrange chicken breast halves in a 12x7½x2-inch baking dish.

● Sprinkle green onions and tarragon atop chicken breasts. Dot chicken with butter or margarine; season with salt and pepper. Add white wine or chicken broth to baking dish.

● Bake, uncovered, in a 350° oven for 30 minutes; remove from oven. In a mixer bowl beat egg white with an electic mixer till stiff peaks form (tips stand straight). Fold mayonnaise or salad dressing into stiffly beaten egg white. Spoon egg white mixture over the chicken breasts. Sprinkle with Parmesan cheese. Return to oven. Bake, uncovered, for 12 to 15 minutes more or till lightly browned.

● Before serving, sprinkle the chicken breasts with the snipped parsley. Makes 4 servings.

1 Skinning chicken breast halves

To remove the skin from the chicken pieces, place one chicken breast half on a cutting surface, skin side up. Holding the chicken breast firmly with one hand, grasp the skin with the other hand and pull it away from the meat; discard the skin.

   Repeat with remaining chicken breast halves.

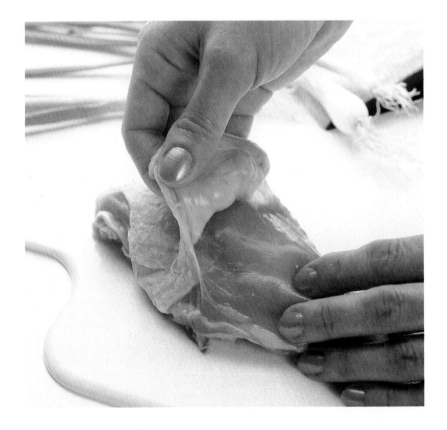

2 Boning the chicken breast halves

Begin boning by holding the chicken breast half on the cutting surface with the bone side down, as shown.

Starting from the breastbone side of the chicken breast, cut the meat away from the bone using a thin, sharp knife. Cut as close to the bone as possible.

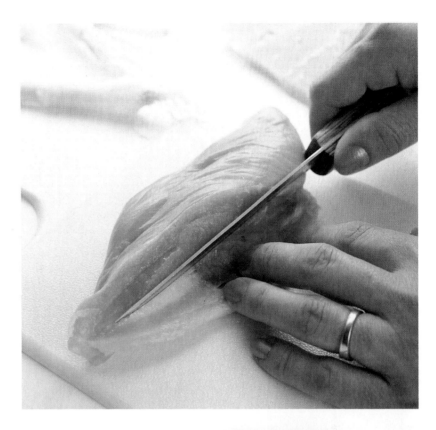

3 Using a sawing motion, continue cutting the meat away from the bone. As you cut, use your free hand to gently pull the rib bones away from the meat.

Repeat steps 2 and 3 with the remaining chicken breast halves; discard all the chicken bones.

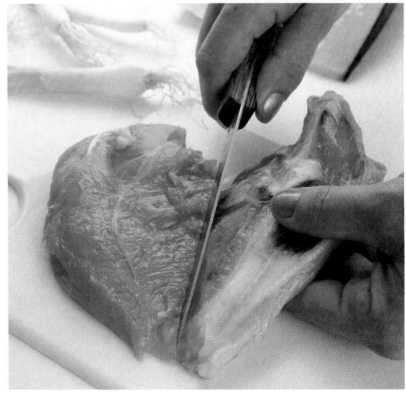

Chilled Salmon Steaks
with Dressing

Chilled Salmon Steaks with Dressing

The refreshing cottage cheese dressing accents these poached salmon steaks.

4 fresh *or* frozen salmon
　steaks, cut ¾ inch thick
　(about 1½ pounds total)
　Cooking oil
1 cup dry white wine
2 *or* 3 sprigs parsley
1 bay leaf
2 tablespoons thinly sliced
　green onion
¼ teaspoon dried thyme,
　crushed
¼ teaspoon dried tarragon,
　crushed
⅔ cup cream-style cottage
　cheese with chives
2 tablespoons snipped parsley
1 tablespoon grated
　Parmesan cheese
1 teaspoon lemon juice
1 to 2 tablespoons milk
　Shredded lettuce (optional)

● Place fresh or thawed steaks in a lightly oiled 10-inch skillet. Add wine, parsley sprigs, and bay leaf to skillet. Sprinkle sliced green onion, thyme, and tarragon over salmon steaks in skillet. Cover and simmer till salmon flakes easily when tested with a fork (see photograph, page 24). (Allow 6 to 8 minutes for fresh fish; 8 to 10 minutes for frozen fish.)

● Carefully remove salmon steaks from skillet; discard poaching liquid in skillet. Refrigerate steaks about 2 hours or till thoroughly chilled.

● For dressing, place cottage cheese, the 2 tablespoons snipped parsley, Parmesan cheese, and lemon juice in a blender container or food processor bowl. Cover; blend or process till smooth. Stir in milk to desired consistency.

● Serve chilled salmon steaks on a bed of shredded lettuce, if desired. Dollop each steak with dressing. Makes 4 servings.

Easy Oven-Fried Fish

Our Test Kitchen taste panel especially liked the tangy citrus flavor of the frozen concentrate and the slight nuttiness of the wheat germ.

1 pound fresh *or* frozen sole
　or flounder fillets
1 slightly beaten egg white
3 tablespoons frozen
　grapefruit *or* orange juice
　concentrate, thawed
1 tablespoon Worcestershire
　sauce
½ cup crushed rich round
　crackers (about 12
　crackers)
¼ cup toasted wheat germ
1 tablespoon butter *or*
　margarine, melted

● Thaw fish, if frozen. Separate the fillets; pat fillets dry with paper toweling.

● Combine beaten egg white, grapefruit or orange juice concentrate, and Worcestershire sauce. Combine the crushed crackers and wheat germ.

● Dip fish fillets in the egg white mixture, then in the crumb mixture. Arrange fillets in a 13x9x2-inch baking dish, tucking under any thin edges so fish will be uniform in thickness and cook evenly.

● Drizzle the melted butter or margarine evenly over fish. Bake in a 500° oven for 8 to 10 minutes or till fish flakes easily when tested with a fork (see photograph, page 24). Makes 4 servings.

Citrus-Marinated Fillets

When buying blocks of frozen fish, make sure they're solidly frozen and that the package sides are straight, not curved in or out. The package should be tightly sealed and show no signs of frost.

1 **pound fresh *or* frozen fish fillets**
⅓ **cup water**
⅓ **cup lime juice**
2 **tablespoons honey**
1 **tablespoon cooking oil**
½ **teaspoon dried dillweed**
¼ **teaspoon salt**

● Thaw fish, if frozen. Separate fillets or cut into 4 serving-size portions. Place fish in a shallow pan.
● For marinade, combine the water, lime juice, honey, cooking oil, dried dillweed, and salt. Pour marinade over fish portions. Cover and refrigerate for 3 to 24 hours; turn fish occasionally.
● Remove the fish from the pan, reserving marinade. Place the fish on the greased rack of an unheated broiler pan, tucking under any thin edges so the fish will be uniform in thickness and cook evenly.
● Broil fish 4 inches from heat till fish flakes easily when tested with a fork (see photograph, below). (Allow 5 minutes for each ½ inch of thickness; if fish pieces are more than 1 inch thick, turn halfway through cooking time.) Baste fish often with reserved marinade during broiling. Brush fish with marinade just before serving. Makes 4 servings.

Testing fish for doneness
To check fish for doneness, insert fork tines into the fish at a 45-degree angle. Twist the fork gently. At the just-done stage, the fish will flake apart easily, as shown, and the flesh will be opaque white.

If fish resists flaking and still has a translucent, pinkish white color, it is not done. A dry and mealy texture indicates that the fish is overcooked.

Wine-Poached Fish with Vegetable Sauce

The sauce is made by reducing the poaching liquid. This process, which involves boiling down the liquid to decrease the amount and to concentrate the flavors, makes a richer tasting sauce.

Cooking oil
¾ cup dry white wine
½ cup water
1 cup sliced fresh mushrooms
½ cup thinly sliced carrots
¼ cup thinly sliced celery
1½ teaspoons instant chicken bouillon granules
½ teaspoon dried rosemary, crushed
4 fresh *or* frozen halibut steaks *or* other fish steaks (1 to 1½ pounds total)

● For poaching liquid, in a lightly oiled 10-inch skillet combine dry white wine and water. Stir in mushrooms, carrots, celery, bouillon granules, and rosemary. Bring to boiling; reduce heat. Simmer, covered, for 5 minutes.

● Add fresh or frozen fish to skillet. Spoon poaching liquid over fish. Simmer, covered, till fish flakes easily when tested with a fork (see photograph, opposite). (Allow 6 to 8 minutes for fresh fish; 8 to 10 minutes for frozen fish.) Using a slotted spoon, transfer the fish and vegetables to a platter; keep warm.

● Boil the poaching liquid, uncovered, about 5 minutes or till reduced to about ⅓ cup. Spoon atop fish and vegetables. Makes 4 servings.

Poaching fish

For poaching the halibut steaks, bring the poaching liquid to a boil, then reduce the heat and simmer, covered, for 5 minutes. This allows the flavors in the poaching liquid to develop.

Gently lower the fish steaks into the poaching liquid, using a spoon or a pancake turner. Spoon the poaching liquid over the fish to moisten the surface, as shown.

Simmer, covered, till the fish tests done when tested with a fork. Use a slotted spoon or pancake turner to remove the cooked fish and vegetables from the skillet so you can reduce the poaching liquid to make the sauce.

Easy Broiled Shrimp

These big shrimp make a great a main dish, but you can also feature them as an appetizer at your next dinner party.

2 pounds fresh *or* frozen large shrimp in shells
½ cup frozen orange juice concentrate
3 tablespoons soy sauce
2 tablespoons cooking oil
¼ teaspoon ground ginger
1 clove garlic, minced

● Thaw shrimp, if frozen. Remove shells and devein the fresh or thawed shrimp.

● For marinade, combine orange juice concentrate, soy sauce, cooking oil, ground ginger, and garlic. Place shrimp in a plastic bag. Pour marinade over the shrimp; close bag. Marinate at room temperature about 1 hour, turning bag occasionally. Remove shrimp from marinade, draining shrimp well. Reserve the marinade.

● To broil, place shrimp on the well-greased rack of an unheated broiler pan. Broil 4 to 5 inches from heat for 4 minutes. Turn shrimp and brush with reserved marinade. Broil for 3 to 4 minutes more or till shrimp are done.

● (Or, to grill, thread shrimp on skewers and grill over *hot* coals for 5 minutes. Turn and brush with reserved marinade. Grill for 5 to 6 minutes more or till done.) Makes 6 servings.

Pasta with Scallop and Wine Sauce

For a different presentation, try tossing the scallop and wine sauce with spinach pasta, instead of plain pasta.

12 ounces fresh *or* frozen scallops
¼ cup chopped onion
1 clove garlic, minced
1 tablespoon butter *or* margarine
½ cup dry white wine
1 teaspoon dried basil, crushed
¼ teaspoon salt
¼ teaspoon dried oregano, crushed
1 tablespoon cold water
2 teaspoons cornstarch
2 medium tomatoes, seeded and chopped (about 1 cup)
6 ounces hot cooked spaghetti, fettuccine, *or* linguine
¼ cup grated Parmesan cheese
2 tablespoons snipped parsley

● Thaw scallops, if frozen. Halve any large scallops. In a saucepan cook onion and garlic in butter or margarine till tender but not brown. Stir in wine, basil, salt, and oregano. Bring to boiling; add scallops. Return to boiling.

● Meanwhile, stir together water and cornstarch. Stir cornstarch mixture into boiling scallop mixture. Cook and stir till thickened and bubbly. Cook and stir for 2 minutes more. Scallops should be opaque. Stir in chopped tomatoes.

● Toss hot cooked spaghetti, fettuccine, or linguine with scallop mixture, Parmesan cheese, and parsley. Makes 4 servings.

Omelets, Soufflés, and Quiches

These pleasing egg dishes will keep your meals light and be anything but dull! Many are filled with a combination of seafood, vegetables, or cheese—favorite foods that will make this collage of first-class recipes some of the most-requested at your house.

Puffy Vegetable Omelet

1 cup chopped zucchini *or* yellow crookneck squash
1 cup sliced fresh mushrooms
1 medium tomato, seeded and chopped
2 tablespoons sliced green onion
1 tablespoon snipped parsley
½ teaspoon dried oregano, crushed
4 egg yolks
¼ teaspoon dried oregano, crushed
4 egg whites
2 tablespoons water
3 tablespoons butter *or* margarine
½ cup shredded cheddar cheese (2 ounces)

● Combine zucchini, mushrooms, tomato, green onion, parsley, and the ½ teaspoon oregano. Set aside.
● Beat the egg yolks and the ¼ teaspoon oregano with an electric mixer on high speed about 5 minutes or till thick and lemon colored. In a large bowl beat egg whites and water till frothy. Continue beating for 1½ to 2 minutes or till stiff peaks form (tips stand straight). Pour beaten egg yolks over egg whites. Gently fold yolks into whites.
● In a 10-inch skillet with an oven-proof handle, heat *1 tablespoon* of the butter or margarine till it sizzles. Lift and tilt skillet to coat sides. Pour egg mixture into hot skillet, mounding it slightly higher around edges. Cook over low heat about 6 minutes or till eggs are puffed and set and bottom is golden brown.
● Place skillet in a 325° oven; bake for 8 to 10 minutes or till a knife inserted between center and edge comes out clean.
● Meanwhile, melt remaining 2 tablespoons butter; add vegetable mixture. Cover; simmer for 3 to 4 minutes or till almost tender. Uncover; cook for 3 minutes more. Drain; keep warm.
● Loosen sides of omelet with a spatula. Make a shallow cut across omelet, cutting slightly off center; fill with vegetable mixture. Fold smaller portion of omelet over larger portion. Sprinkle with cheese. Serve immediately. Makes 2 servings.

Cutting Back on Sugar and Fat

Concerned about the amounts of sugar and fat in your diet? You'll be able to reduce your sugar intake if you work these practices into your daily routine:
● Serve more *fresh* fruit. Remember that the syrup in many *canned* fruits is extremely high in sugar.
● Try drinking fruit juices instead of soft drinks.
● Always check the labels on processed foods. Avoid foods with sugar high on the list of ingredients.

The following ideas will help you cut down on the amount of fat you eat:
● Choose *lean* meats; include more fish and poultry (without skin) when planning menus.
● Stay away from fried foods. Also, drain off as much fat as possible after cooking.
● Try using skim, 1%, or 2% milk. Eat low-fat yogurt and low-fat cottage cheese.

Puffy Vegetable Omelet

Ham-Filled Omelets

If you think omelets are strictly breakfast food, we bet you'll change your mind when you try one of these satisfying omelets for supper.

½ cup sliced fresh mushrooms
1 tablespoon chopped onion
1 tablespoon chopped green pepper
¼ cup water
½ cup cubed fully cooked ham
2 teaspoons horseradish mustard
4 eggs
2 tablespoons water
    Dash pepper
2 teaspoons butter *or* margarine
¼ cup shredded Swiss cheese
    Snipped chives (optional)

● For filling, cook mushrooms, onion, and green pepper in the ¼ cup water about 5 minutes or till tender; drain. Stir in ham and horseradish mustard; set filling aside.

● For omelets, beat together with a fork the eggs, the 2 tablespoons water, and pepper till blended but not frothy. In a 6- or 8-inch skillet with flared sides, heat *1 teaspoon* of the butter or margarine till it sizzles. Lift and tilt skillet to coat sides. Pour *half* of the egg mixture into skillet; cook over medium heat.

● As eggs set, run a narrow spatula around edges of skillet, lifting the eggs to allow uncooked portion to flow underneath. When eggs are set but still slightly shiny, remove from heat.

● Spoon *half* of the filling across the center of the omelet. Fold one-third of the omelet over the center. Overlap the remaining one-third over the center. Slide the filled omelet from the skillet onto an oven-proof plate. Keep omelet warm in a 200° oven while preparing second omelet.

● For second omelet, repeat cooking, using the remaining 1 teaspoon butter, egg mixture, and filling. Sprinkle omelets with cheese. Garnish with chives, if desired. Makes 2 servings.

1 Making an omelet
When making an omelet, use a skillet with flared sides, because this type of edge makes it easier to slide the cooked omelet out of the pan. However, a straight-sided skillet also may be used.

Pour the egg mixture into the heated skillet. Cook over medium heat.

As the eggs begin to set, run a metal spatula or pancake turner around the edges of the skillet, lifting the eggs to let the uncooked portion flow underneath, as shown. If you like, tip the pan slightly so eggs flow easily. Don't stir mixture at this point or you could end up with scrambled eggs.

2 Remove the skillet from the heat when the eggs are set but still slightly shiny on the top surface. Be careful not to cook the eggs longer, because overcooking will give them a tough, rubbery texture.

Spoon about *half* of the filling across the center of the cooked omelet, as shown.

3 Using a spatula or a pancake turner, carefully lift one-third of the cooked omelet and fold it over the filling in the center. Then carefully lift the remaining one-third of the omelet and overlap it over the center.

To remove the filled omelet from the skillet, gently slide it to the edge of the skillet. Tilt the skillet, then invert it so the omelet rolls out onto an oven-proof plate.

Spinach-Mushroom Soufflé Roll

Spinach-Mushroom Soufflé Roll

Serve this appealing "rolled-up" version of a soufflé the next time dinner guests are at your house.

¼ cup butter *or* margarine
½ cup all-purpose flour
½ teaspoon salt
  Dash pepper
2 cups milk
6 egg yolks
¼ cup grated Parmesan cheese
6 egg whites
¼ teaspoon cream of tartar
  Spinach-Mushroom Filling

● Line a 15x10x1-inch baking pan with foil, extending foil 1 inch beyond edges of pan. Grease and lightly flour; set aside.
● Melt the butter or margarine. Stir in the ½ cup flour, salt, and pepper. Add milk all at once. Cook and stir till thickened and bubbly. Cook and stir 1 minute more. Remove from heat.
● Beat the egg yolks till thick and lemon colored. *Slowly* stir thickened milk mixture and Parmesan cheese into beaten egg yolks. Using clean beaters, beat egg whites and cream of tartar till stiff peaks form. Fold a small amount of the beaten egg whites into egg yolk mixture. Fold egg yolk mixture into remaining egg whites; spread in prepared pan. Bake in a 375° oven about 20 minutes or till puffed and slightly set. Immediately loosen from pan; turn out onto foil. Spread Spinach-Mushroom Filling over soufflé to within ½ inch of edges. Use foil to start rolling up soufflé jelly-roll style, beginning with one of the short sides. Slice; serve immediately. Makes 4 servings.

Spinach-Mushroom Filling: Cook one 10-ounce package frozen chopped *spinach* according to package directions; drain well. Meanwhile, cook ½ cup sliced fresh *mushrooms* and 1 tablespoon finely chopped *onion* in 1 tablespoon *butter or margarine* till tender but not brown. Stir in cooked and well-drained spinach, one 3-ounce package softened *cream cheese*, 1 tablespoon Dijon-style *mustard*, and ¼ teaspoon ground *nutmeg*. Heat through, stirring occasionally.

Vegetable-Cheese Soufflé

¾ cup thinly sliced carrots
¼ cup butter *or* margarine
¼ cup all-purpose flour
¼ teaspoon salt
  Dash pepper
1 cup milk
1 cup shredded cheddar
    cheese (4 ounces)
1 cup shredded parsnips,
    potatoes, turnips, *or*
    rutabagas
6 egg yolks
6 egg whites

● Cook carrots, covered, in a small amount of boiling water for 15 to 20 minutes or till tender. Drain; mash carrots with a fork. (You should have about ½ cup mashed carrots.) Set aside.
● Attach a foil collar to a 2- or 2½-quart soufflé dish (see photograph, page 34). Set dish aside.
● Melt butter or margarine. Stir in flour, salt, and pepper. Add milk all at once. Cook and stir till thickened and bubbly. Cook and stir 1 minute more. Remove from heat; add shredded cheese, stirring till melted. Stir in carrots and parsnips, potatoes, turnips, or rutabagas.
● Beat egg yolks till thick and lemon colored. *Slowly* stir in vegetable mixture. Using clean beaters, beat egg whites till stiff peaks form. Fold vegetable mixture into beaten whites. Turn into prepared soufflé dish. Bake in a 325° oven for 55 to 60 minutes or till a knife inserted between center and edge comes out clean. Peel off collar; serve immediately. Makes 4 servings.

Spinach, Shrimp, and Cheese Soufflé

Specks of green from the spinach and pink from the shrimp color this rich-tasting soufflé.

¼ cup butter *or* margarine
¼ cup all-purpose flour
¾ cup milk
½ cup grated Parmesan cheese
¼ cup dry white wine
1 cup finely chopped fresh
    spinach
1 4½-ounce can shrimp,
    rinsed, drained, and finely
    chopped
5 egg yolks
5 egg whites

● Attach a foil collar to a 1½-quart soufflé dish (see photograph, below). Set dish aside.

● In a saucepan melt the butter or margarine; stir in flour. Add milk all at once. Cook and stir till thickened and bubbly. Cook and stir 1 minute more. Remove from heat. Stir in Parmesan cheese and white wine. Fold in chopped spinach and finely chopped shrimp.

● Beat egg yolks till thick and lemon colored. *Slowly* stir in spinach mixture. Using clean beaters, beat egg whites till stiff peaks form (tips stand straight). Fold spinach mixture into the beaten egg whites.

● Turn mixture into prepared 1½-quart soufflé dish. Bake in a 325° oven for 50 to 55 minutes or till a knife inserted between center and edge comes out clean. Gently peel off collar. Serve soufflé immediately. Makes 4 servings.

Attaching a foil collar to a soufflé dish

Because soufflés climb as they bake, a collar around the dish keeps the mixture from spilling over the sides. To make a collar, measure enough foil to go around the dish, plus a 2- to 3-inch overlap. Fold foil into thirds lengthwise; butter one side.

With the buttered side in, position the foil around the outside of the dish, letting the collar extend about 2 inches above the top of the dish; fasten with tape.

After turning mixture into dish, use a knife to trace a 1-inch-deep circle through mixture, about 1 inch from edge of dish. As soufflé bakes, a "top hat" will form.

Shrimp and Broccoli Quiche

A Test Kitchen tip: Lining the pastry shell with foil during baking prevents the crust from puffing up or shrinking.

½ cup frozen cut broccoli
3 beaten eggs
1½ cups milk
3 tablespoons sliced green onion
⅔ cup chopped, cooked, fresh *or* frozen shrimp
1½ cups shredded Swiss cheese (6 ounces)
1 tablespoon all-purpose flour
Whole Wheat Pastry Shell
Parsley sprigs (optional)

● To thaw frozen broccoli, put it in a colander and rinse under hot tap water. Drain well; set broccoli aside.

● Stir together beaten eggs, milk, and green onion; stir in shrimp. Toss together shredded Swiss cheese and flour; stir into egg mixture. Stir in broccoli.

● Prepare the Whole Wheat Pastry Shell. Pour egg mixture into the *hot* baked pastry shell.

● Bake in a 325° oven for 40 to 45 minutes or till a knife inserted between center and edge comes out clean. If necessary, cover the edge of the crust with foil during baking to prevent overbrowning.

● Let quiche stand for 5 to 10 minutes before serving. Garnish with parsley sprigs, if desired. Makes 6 servings.

Whole Wheat Pastry Shell: In a mixing bowl stir together ¾ cup *whole wheat flour,* ½ cup *all-purpose flour,* and ½ teaspoon *salt.* Cut in ⅓ cup *shortening or lard* till pieces are the size of small peas. Sprinkle 1 tablespoon *cold milk* over part of the mixture; gently toss with a fork. Push to side of bowl. Repeat with 2 to 3 tablespoons additional milk till all is moistened. Form dough into a ball.

● On a lightly floured surface flatten dough with hands. Roll dough from center to edge, forming a circle about 12 inches in diameter. Wrap pastry around a rolling pin; unroll onto a 9-inch pie plate. Ease pastry into pie plate, being careful not to stretch pastry. Trim to ½ inch beyond edge of pie plate; fold under extra pastry. Flute edge.

● Line the unpricked pastry shell with a double thickness of heavy-duty foil. Bake in a 450° oven for 5 minutes. Remove foil; bake about 5 minutes more or till pastry is nearly done. Remove pastry from oven. Reduce oven temperature to 325°.

Crustless Quiche Lorraine

We've "lightened" this classic recipe by eliminating the pastry crust.

2 teaspoons butter *or* margarine
2 tablespoons toasted wheat germ
4 slices bacon
3 tablespoons sliced green onion
5 beaten eggs
1¼ cups milk
⅛ teaspoon ground red pepper
1 cup shredded Swiss *or* Gruyère cheese (4 ounces)

● Grease a 9-inch pie plate or quiche dish with the butter or margarine. Sprinkle the wheat germ over the bottom and up the sides of the pie plate or quiche dish; set aside.
● Cook the bacon till crisp; drain, reserving 1 tablespoon drippings. Crumble the bacon; set aside. Cook the green onion in the reserved drippings till tender; drain well.
● Stir together the eggs, milk, and ground red pepper. Stir in the crumbled bacon, cooked green onion, and the shredded Swiss or Gruyère cheese; mix well.
● Pour the egg mixture into the prepared pie plate or quiche dish. Bake in a 325° oven for 30 to 35 minutes or till a knife inserted between center and edge comes out clean. Let stand 5 to 10 minutes before serving. Makes 6 servings.

Apples 'n' Cheddar Quiche

This recipe started out using sliced apples, but when we found them difficult to eat, we switched to the chopped apples.

1 cup chopped cooking apples
3 beaten eggs
1½ cups milk
¼ teaspoon ground nutmeg
1½ cups shredded cheddar cheese (6 ounces)
1 tablespoon all-purpose flour
Pastry Shell

● Cook chopped apples in a small amount of boiling water for 2 to 3 minutes or just till tender. Drain; set aside.
● Stir together beaten eggs, milk, and nutmeg. Toss together cheddar cheese and flour; stir into egg mixture. Add apple.
● Prepare Pastry Shell. Pour egg mixture into *hot* baked pastry shell. Bake in a 325° oven for 35 to 40 minutes or till a knife inserted between center and edge comes out clean. If necessary, cover edge with foil during baking to prevent overbrowning. Let stand 5 to 10 minutes before serving. Makes 6 servings.

Pastry Shell: In a mixing bowl stir together 1¼ cups *all-purpose flour* and ½ teaspoon *salt*. Cut in ⅓ cup *shortening or lard* till pieces are the size of small peas. Sprinkle 1 tablespoon *cold water* over part of the mixture; gently toss with a fork. Push to side of bowl. Repeat with 3 to 4 tablespoons additional water till all is moistened. Form dough into a ball.
● On a lightly floured surface flatten dough with hands. Roll from center to edge, forming a circle about 12 inches in diameter. Wrap pastry around rolling pin; unroll onto a 9-inch pie plate. Ease pastry into plate. Trim to ½ inch beyond edge of pie plate; fold under extra pastry. Flute edge.
● Line unpricked pastry shell with a double thickness of heavy-duty foil. Bake in a 450° oven for 5 minutes. Remove foil. Bake about 5 minutes more or till pastry is nearly done. Remove from oven. Reduce oven temperature to 325°.

Wholesome Main-Dish Salads

Filled with fruits and vegetables, meat, poultry, seafood, cheese, or greens, these main-dish salads are truly feasts in themselves. Most of the salads have accompanying dressings that help add to the uniqueness of every recipe, but you'll find they *all* abound with freshness and a variety of satisfying flavors, colors, and textures.

Chicken, Shrimp, and Fruit Salad

Since fresh cantaloupe and honeydew melon are in season at the same time, alternate using one or the other in this main-dish salad.

2 cups cubed cooked
   chicken *or* turkey
1 cup seedless green grapes,
   halved
1 cup cubed cantaloupe *or*
   honeydew melon
1 8-ounce can sliced water
   chestnuts, drained
1 4½-ounce can shrimp,
   rinsed and drained
1 small banana
⅓ cup mayonnaise *or* salad
   dressing
1 tablespoon lemon juice
   Lettuce leaves (optional)

● For salad, in a large bowl combine cooked chicken or turkey, halved grapes, cubed cantaloupe or honeydew melon, water chestnuts, and shrimp. Cover and chill for several hours.

● For dressing, in a small bowl mash the banana. Stir in the mayonnaise or salad dressing and the lemon juice. Cover; chill for several hours.

● If desired, arrange lettuce leaves on plates. Serve salad atop lettuce. Drizzle with dressing. Makes 6 servings.

Chicken-Sesame Salad

The radishes add crispness to the salad, as well as a peppery flavor.

2 tablespoons salad oil
2 tablespoons vinegar
1 tablespoon sesame seed,
   toasted
1 teaspoon sugar
¼ teaspoon salt
⅛ teaspoon pepper
4 cups torn salad greens
2 cups cooked chicken *or*
   turkey, cut into bite-size
   strips
5 radishes, sliced
2 green onions, sliced
1 hard-cooked egg, cut
   into wedges

● For dressing, in a screw-top jar combine salad oil, vinegar, sesame seed, sugar, salt, and pepper. Cover and shake well to mix. Chill thoroughly.

● For salad, in a large salad bowl combine torn salad greens, cooked chicken or turkey, sliced radishes, and sliced green onions. Toss lightly.

● Shake dressing again just before serving. Pour dressing over salad; toss lightly to coat. Garnish with the hard-cooked egg wedges. Makes 4 servings.

Chicken, Shrimp, and
Fruit Salad

Chicken-Avocado Salad

Chilling the salad and dressing separately prevents the rice in the salad from absorbing too much of the dressing.

3 cups cooked rice
3 cups chopped cooked chicken
½ cup thinly sliced celery
¼ cup thinly sliced green onion
1 medium avocado
⅓ cup mayonnaise *or* salad dressing
¼ cup milk
2 tablespoons vinegar
1 teaspoon dried parsley flakes
⅛ teaspoon salt
Lettuce leaves
Avocado slices (optional)
Tomato wedges (optional)

● In a large bowl combine the cooked rice, chopped chicken, sliced celery, and sliced green onion. Cover the rice mixture; chill for several hours.

● Use a sharp knife to cut the avocado in half lengthwise. Twist the avocado gently to separate the two halves. Tap the seed with the blade of the knife so the blade remains in the seed. Twist and gently lift out the seed. Use the sharp knife to peel the halved avocado.

● For the dressing, mash the avocado pulp. Stir in the mayonnaise or salad dressing, milk, vinegar, parsley flakes, and salt. Cover and chill for several hours.

● Just before serving, pour the dressing over the rice mixture; toss lightly to coat. Arrange lettuce leaves on plates. Serve the salad atop lettuce. Garnish with avocado slices and tomato wedges, if desired. Makes 6 servings.

How to "Julienne"

In many salad recipes, you'll notice that some of the ingredients need to be cut into "julienne strips." Just what is this cut and how do you do it?

To "julienne" meats and vegetables means to cut them into long thin strips.

Start by cutting a thin slice off one side of the meat or vegetable, if necessary, so it will lie flat on the cutting surface. Placing the flat side down, cut the food into lengthwise slices. Then cut each slice into narrow strips about ⅛ to ¼ inch thick.

Selecting and preparing an avocado

For best flavor, an avocado must be ripe before you use it in this salad. To test ripeness, cradle the avocado in the palm of your hand; if it yields to gentle pressure, it's ready to use. If some feeling of firmness remains, however, keep the avocado at room temperature till it reaches the desired softness. You may store a ripe avocado in the refrigerator for up to three days.

To prepare the avocado, cut the fruit lengthwise around the seed. Gently twist the halves in opposite directions to separate.

To remove the seed from the avocado, carefully tap the seed with the blade of a sharp knife so the blade is caught in the seed. Rotate the knife to loosen the seed, then use the knife to lift the seed out. (This method of removing the seed lessens the bruising of the avocado.)

To peel the avocado, place the cut side down in your palm. Use the sharp knife to loosen and strip the skin from the fruit.

41

Cinnamon Chicken Salad in Tomato Cups

Doll up your regular lunch menu with this easy, yet special salad.

3 cups chopped cooked
    chicken *or* turkey
½ cup chopped celery
½ cup chopped pecans
¼ cup dried currants *or* raisins
½ cup plain yogurt
⅓ cup mayonnaise *or* salad
    dressing
2 tablespoons snipped parsley
2 teaspoons lime juice
½ teaspoon salt
¼ teaspoon ground cinnamon
    Tomato Cups
    Lettuce leaves

● For salad, combine chicken or turkey, celery, pecans, and currants or raisins.

● For dressing, stir together yogurt, mayonnaise or salad dressing, parsley, lime juice, salt, and cinnamon. Pour dressing over salad; toss lightly to coat. Cover salad mixture and chill for several hours.

● To serve, place chilled Tomato Cups on individual lettuce-lined plates. Spreading the wedges apart, fill *each* Tomato Cup with about ⅔ cup of the salad mixture. Makes 6 servings.

Tomato Cups: Place 6 medium *tomatoes,* stem end down, on a cutting surface. With a sharp knife, cut each tomato into 4 to 6 wedges, cutting to, but not through the base of the tomato. Spread the wedges apart slightly. Cover and chill.

Curried Salmon Salad

Adjust the curry level to your taste by using either the lower or higher amount of seasoning.

1 15½-ounce can red salmon
1 banana, sliced
1 medium apple, chopped
    (1 cup)
    Lemon juice
1½ cups cooked rice
1 small green pepper, cut into
    1½-inch strips
½ cup mayonnaise *or* salad
    dressing
2 tablespoons milk
1½ to 2 teaspoons curry powder
    Lettuce leaves

● Remove skin and bones from salmon; break salmon into chunks. Set aside.

● For salad, in a large bowl toss banana and chopped apple with a little lemon juice; stir in salmon, cooked rice, and green pepper strips. Cover; chill for several hours.

● For dressing, in a small bowl combine mayonnaise or salad dressing, milk, and curry powder. Cover; chill for several hours.

● Just before serving, pour dressing over salad; toss lightly to coat. Transfer salmon salad mixture to a lettuce-lined salad bowl. Makes 4 servings.

Cabbage-Tuna Toss

When buying a head of cabbage, you can plan on one pound yielding about 5 cups of raw, coarsely shredded cabbage.

3	cups shredded cabbage
1	6½-ounce can tuna (water pack), drained and broken into chunks
¾	cup sliced fresh mushrooms
1	medium tomato, cut into thin wedges
½	of a medium cucumber, thinly sliced
12	pitted ripe olives, halved lengthwise
6	radishes, thinly sliced
⅓	cup mayonnaise *or* salad dressing
⅓	cup plain yogurt
2	teaspoons prepared mustard
¾	teaspoon dried dillweed

● For salad, in a large salad bowl combine shredded cabbage, tuna, mushrooms, tomato wedges, cucumber, ripe olives, and radishes. Cover salad; chill for several hours.

● For dressing, in a small bowl stir together mayonnaise or salad dressing, plain yogurt, prepared mustard, and dillweed. Cover; chill for several hours.

● Just before serving, pour dressing over salad; toss lightly to coat. Makes 4 servings.

Shredding cabbage

You can vary the size and texture of cabbage shreds simply by using different methods to cut the cabbage.

For long, coarse shreds, hold a quarter-head of cabbage firmly against a cutting surface; cut into even shreds with a long-bladed knife, as shown.

For shorter, medium shreds, push a quarter-head of cabbage across the coarse blade of a vegetable shredder.

For fine, juicy shreds, cut the cabbage into small wedges. Fill the blender about ½ full; cover with cold water. Cover and blend just till chopped; drain well.

Ham and Fruit Toss

Shrimp Salad

A tart citrus dressing wakes up this colorful salad.

1 16-ounce can orange and
 grapefruit sections
2 6-ounce packages frozen
 cooked shrimp
3 cups torn leaf lettuce
1 cup frozen crinkle-cut
 carrots, thawed
½ of a small onion, thinly
 sliced and separated
 into rings
 Dash pepper
 Citrus Dressing

● Drain orange and grapefruit sections, reserving 2 table-spoons juice for the dressing. To thaw shrimp, place shrimp in a colander under cool running water for 1 to 2 minutes or till thawed. Set shrimp aside to drain.

● For salad, in a large salad bowl place torn leaf lettuce, thawed carrots, onion rings, pepper, drained orange and grapefruit sections, and thawed shrimp. Toss lightly.

● Pour Citrus Dressing over the salad; toss lightly to coat. Makes 4 servings.

Citrus Dressing: In a screw-top jar combine ¼ cup *salad oil;* 2 tablespoons *lemon or lime juice;* ¼ teaspoon dried *tarragon or basil, crushed;* dash *paprika;* and *the reserved 2 tablespoons juice.* Cover and shake well to mix. Chill. Shake dressing again just before serving.

Ham and Fruit Toss

Transforming a hollowed-out pineapple into a serving bowl gives a tropical touch to your salad. (Pictured on the cover.)

2 small fresh pineapples,
 chilled
3 cups torn romaine
1 cup cubed fully cooked ham
1 orange, sectioned
2 ounces Swiss cheese, cut
 into julienne strips
1 8-ounce carton plain yogurt
2 tablespoons orange juice

● Use a sharp knife to halve the fresh pineapples lengthwise, crown and all. Remove hard core from pineapple. Cut out pineapple meat, leaving shells intact. Set shells aside.

● Remove eyes from the pineapple meat. Cut pineapple into chunks, reserving 3 cups (refrigerate remaining pineapple for another use).

● For salad, combine torn romaine, cubed ham, orange sections, Swiss cheese, and reserved pineapple chunks; toss lightly. Spoon into pineapple shells.

● For dressing, stir together yogurt and orange juice. Serve dressing with salads. Makes 4 servings.

Tabouleh-Seafood Salad

Turn Middle Eastern tabouleh salad into a full-size meal by tossing it with shrimp and clams.

2 cups warm water
¾ cup bulgur wheat
1 10-ounce can whole baby clams, drained
1 6-ounce package frozen cooked shrimp, thawed
1 4-ounce can sliced mushrooms, drained
2 red *or* green sweet peppers, cut into ½-inch squares
¼ cup olive *or* salad oil
2 tablespoons lemon juice
½ teaspoon dried dillweed
¼ teaspoon salt
Lettuce leaves
2 medium tomatoes, sliced and halved
½ of a small onion, thinly sliced and separated into rings

● For salad, in a bowl combine the warm water and bulgur. Let stand for 1 hour. Drain well; press excess water out of bulgur. Combine the bulgur, clams, shrimp, mushrooms, and red or green sweet peppers.

● For dressing, in a screw-top jar combine olive or salad oil, lemon juice, dillweed, and salt. Cover and shake well to mix. Pour dressing over salad; toss lightly to coat. Cover and chill for several hours.

● Just before serving, spoon salad into a lettuce-lined salad bowl. Arrange tomatoes around edge of bowl. Top with onion rings. Makes 4 servings.

Spicy Beef Salad

The blend of spices used in the marinade gives this salad a zesty, south-of-the-border taste.

⅓ cup wine vinegar
3 tablespoons salad oil
½ teaspoon dried oregano, crushed
½ teaspoon chili powder
¼ teaspoon ground cumin
⅛ teaspoon garlic powder
⅛ teaspoon crushed red pepper
8 ounces cooked lean beef, cut into julienne strips (1½ cups)
2 cups torn lettuce
2 cups torn romaine
1 cup shredded Monterey Jack cheese (4 ounces)
½ cup cherry tomatoes, halved, *or* 1 medium tomato, cut into wedges
2 hard-cooked eggs, sliced

● For marinade, combine the wine vinegar, salad oil, oregano, chili powder, cumin, garlic powder, and crushed red pepper. Place the beef strips in a bowl; pour the marinade over beef. Cover and marinate in the refrigerator for several hours or overnight, stirring occasionally.

● Just before serving, drain beef; reserve the marinade. Place torn lettuce and romaine in a large salad bowl. Top with drained beef strips, shredded cheese, cherry tomato halves or tomato wedges, and hard-cooked eggs. Pour reserved marinade over salad; toss lightly to coat. Makes 6 servings.

Taco Salad

Here are all the makings of a taco—a tortilla, beef, cheese, and lettuce—in a meal-size salad.

Tortilla Bowls
- ¾ pound lean ground beef
- ½ cup chopped onion
- 1 clove garlic, minced
- 1 cup canned whole kernel corn
- 1 8-ounce can tomato sauce
- 1 7½-ounce can tomatoes, cut up
- 1 4-ounce can green chili peppers, rinsed, seeded, and chopped
- 1 tablespoon all-purpose flour
- 2 teaspoons chili powder
- 6 cups torn lettuce
- 1 cup shredded cheddar *or* American cheese
- ¼ cup sliced pitted ripe olives
- 1 tomato, cut into wedges
- 1 green pepper, cut into strips

● Prepare Tortilla Bowls; cool. Remove foil from bowls.

● Cook ground beef, chopped onion, and garlic till meat is browned and onion is tender; drain well. Stir in drained corn, tomato sauce, *undrained* tomatoes, green chili peppers, flour, and chili powder. Cook and stir till thickened and bubbly. Cook and stir 1 minute more.

● Meanwhile, combine lettuce, *¾ cup* of the shredded cheese, and the ripe olives; toss lightly. Place lettuce mixture in Tortilla Bowls. Spoon meat mixture over lettuce mixture.

● Top each salad with tomato wedges and green pepper strips. Sprinkle with remaining cheese. Makes 4 servings.

Tortilla Bowls: Cut eight 10-inch circles from heavy-duty foil. In a large skillet warm four 10-inch *flour tortillas,* one at a time, over low heat about 1 minute or just till warm and pliable. Place *each* warm tortilla on 2 foil circles and shape into a ruffled bowl. Place tortilla bowls on an ungreased baking sheet. Bake in a 350° oven about 10 minutes or till crisp.

Making Tortilla Bowls

Put the lid of a 10-inch skillet on top of eight sheets of heavy-duty foil. Draw around lid, forming a 10-inch circle. Holding foil sheets together, cut out circle.

Warm the tortillas, one at a time, in a skillet over low heat. Heat about one minute or just till warm and pliable.

Put two foil circles together; top with warm tortilla. Shape tortilla and foil together into a ruffled bowl. Repeat with remaining foil circles and tortillas. (The foil acts as a support.)

Place tortilla bowls on an ungreased baking sheet. Bake in a 350° oven about 10 minutes or till crisp. Cool; remove foil. Fill with salad.

Classic Chef's Salad

You won't leave the table hungry after dining on one of these ample salads!

9 cups torn salad greens
6 ounces Swiss *or* cheddar
   cheese, cut into julienne
   strips
3 ounces fully cooked ham *or*
   cooked lean beef, cut into
   julienne strips
6 ounces cooked chicken *or*
   turkey, cut into julienne
   strips
¼ cup crumbled blue cheese,
   crumbled feta cheese, *or*
   grated Parmesan cheese
   (optional)
4 hard-cooked eggs, sliced
2 small green peppers, cut
   into strips
1 small cucumber, thinly
   sliced
1 cup cherry tomatoes, halved
¾ cup sliced radishes
¾ cup Creamy French
   Dressing

● Place the torn salad greens into 6 large individual salad bowls. Arrange Swiss or cheddar cheese strips, ham or beef strips, and chicken or turkey strips over salad greens; sprinkle with blue, feta, or Parmesan cheese, if desired.
● Add the hard-cooked egg slices, green pepper strips, cucumber slices, cherry tomato halves, and radishes. Serve salads with Creamy French Dressing. Makes 6 servings.

Creamy French Dressing: In a small mixer bowl combine 1 tablespoon *paprika*, 2 teaspoons *sugar*, 1 teaspoon *salt*, and dash ground *red pepper*. Add ¼ cup *vinegar* and 1 *egg*; beat well. Add 1 cup *salad oil* in a slow, steady stream, beating constantly with an electric mixer till thick. Cover; store remaining dressing in the refrigerator. Makes about 1⅔ cups.

Preparing Salad Greens

No matter what type of salad greens you buy, they should look fresh and perky. Storing greens in the refrigerator in a sealed plastic bag or crisper container will ensure crispness.

Several hours before using any greens, remove them from the refrigerator and wash them well under cold running water. Shake off any excess water and pat the greens dry with a kitchen towel or paper towel. Return them to the refrigerator to give them time to become crisp.

Tear, don't cut, the greens into bite-size pieces. Tearing exposes the juicy insides and allows dressing to be absorbed by the greens; cutting with a knife hastens darkening of the edges.

Satisfying Soups and Sandwiches

You won't find any ho-hum standbys here. Instead, we've taken a fresh look at two meal-time favorites. We've come up with new and exciting blends of ingredients, as in Chicken-Corn Chowder and Chutney-Turkey Salad Sandwiches—soup and sandwich entrées with enough character to serve as the mainstay of your meal.

Broccoli-Ham Soup

Prepare this elegant soup when unexpected guests arrive—it's ready in minutes.

¼ cup chopped onion
3 tablespoons butter *or* margarine
¼ cup all-purpose flour
1½ teaspoons instant chicken bouillon granules
1 teaspoon dry mustard
½ teaspoon dried thyme, crushed
⅛ teaspoon pepper
2 cups milk
2 cups water
2 cups broccoli flowerets *or* frozen cut broccoli
1½ cups cubed fully cooked ham

● In a 3-quart saucepan cook the chopped onion in butter or margarine till tender but not brown. Stir in flour, chicken bouillon granules, mustard, thyme, and pepper. Add milk and water all at once. Cook and stir over medium-high heat till thickened and bubbly.

● Stir fresh broccoli flowerets or frozen cut broccoli and cubed ham into saucepan. Return to boiling. Reduce heat; simmer for 4 to 6 minutes more or till the broccoli is tender and the soup is heated through, stirring occasionally. Makes 4 servings.

Curried Fish Soup

Serve a bowlful of this easy fish soup with a piece of crusty bread or an assortment of crackers.

1 16-ounce package frozen fish fillets
½ cup chopped onion
½ cup chopped celery
½ cup chopped carrot
2 teaspoons curry powder
2 tablespoons butter *or* margarine
2 14½-ounce cans chicken broth
1½ cups milk
4 teaspoons cornstarch

● Thaw fish at room temperature for 20 minutes. Cut the fish into ½-inch pieces; set aside.

● In a 3-quart saucepan cook the onion, celery, carrot, and curry powder in the butter or margarine till vegetables are tender but not brown.

● Stir in chicken broth all at once. Cook and stir about 5 minutes or till bubbly; stir in pieces of fish. Cook and stir for 4 to 5 minutes more or till fish flakes easily.

● Meanwhile, combine milk and cornstarch. Stir into fish mixture. Cook and stir till thickened and bubbly. Cook and stir 2 minutes more. Makes 6 servings.

Broccoli-Ham Soup

Turkey and Rice Soup

Put your leftover holiday turkey to good use in this convenient meal-in-one soup.

¼ cup chopped onion
¼ cup chopped green pepper
1 clove garlic, minced
3 tablespoons butter *or* margarine
3 tablespoons all-purpose flour
½ teaspoon salt
¼ teaspoon dried marjoram, crushed
¼ teaspoon dried basil, crushed
2½ cups milk
1 14½-ounce can chicken broth
1½ cups chopped cooked turkey *or* chicken
1 10-ounce package frozen peas
1 cup cooked rice
2 medium tomatoes, cut into chunks, *or* 12 cherry tomatoes, halved

● In a 3-quart saucepan cook chopped onion, chopped green pepper, and garlic in butter or margarine till tender but not brown. Stir in flour, salt, marjoram, and basil. Add milk and broth all at once. Cook and stir till thickened and bubbly. Cook and stir for 1 minute more.

● Stir in chopped cooked turkey or chicken, peas, and cooked rice. Cook for 6 to 8 minutes or till heated through, stirring occasionally. Stir in tomato chunks or cherry tomato halves. Cook for 1 minute more. Makes 5 servings.

Chicken-Corn Chowder

To cut fresh corn off the cob, use a sharp knife to cut off just the kernel tips.

2 slices bacon
¼ cup chopped onion
2 cups chicken broth
1 10-ounce package frozen whole kernel corn *or* 2 cups cut fresh corn
2 medium potatoes, peeled and chopped
½ cup chopped celery
½ teaspoon dried savory, crushed
¼ teaspoon pepper
2 cups milk
2 tablespoons all-purpose flour
2 cups chopped cooked chicken *or* turkey

● In a 3-quart saucepan cook the bacon till crisp. Drain bacon, reserving drippings. Crumble bacon and set aside.

● Cook onion in reserved drippings till tender but not brown. Stir in chicken broth, frozen corn or cut fresh corn, chopped potatoes, chopped celery, dried savory, pepper, and ½ teaspoon *salt*. Bring to boiling; reduce heat. Cover and simmer about 15 minutes or till vegetables are tender.

● Meanwhile, combine milk and flour. Stir into vegetable mixture. Cook and stir till thickened and bubbly. Cook and stir 1 minute more. Stir in chopped chicken or turkey; heat through. Top with crumbled bacon. Makes 6 servings.

Minestrone Soup

½ cup chopped onion
½ cup chopped celery
1 clove garlic, minced
1 tablespoon olive *or* cooking oil
3 cups beef broth
1 16-ounce can tomatoes, cut up, *or* 2 tomatoes, peeled and chopped
2 tablespoons snipped parsley
2 teaspoons dried basil, crushed
1 teaspoon dried oregano, crushed
1 bay leaf
2 cups fresh vegetables (any combination of uncooked cubed potatoes, chopped broccoli, *or* sliced carrots)
¾ cup cooked *or* canned red kidney beans
1 ounce spaghetti, broken (about ½ cup)
¼ cup grated Parmesan *or* Romano cheese

● In a 3-quart saucepan cook the chopped onion, chopped celery, and garlic in olive or cooking oil till tender but not brown. Stir in the beef broth, the *undrained* canned tomatoes or the peeled and chopped tomatoes, snipped parsley, basil, oregano, bay leaf, and ¼ teaspoon *pepper.*

● Bring to boiling; reduce heat. Cover and simmer for 30 minutes. Add the 2 cups fresh vegetables. Simmer, covered, about 15 minutes more or till the vegetables are just tender. Stir in the cooked or canned red kidney beans and the broken spaghetti. Cook about 15 minutes more or till the spaghetti is tender, stirring occasionally.

● Remove the bay leaf. Ladle the soup mixture into bowls. Sprinkle each serving with the grated Parmesan or Romano cheese. Makes 4 servings.

Ground Beef and Vegetable Soup

To remove as much excess fat as possible from the cooked ground beef, drain the meat in a colander and pat it dry with paper towels.

1 pound lean ground beef
½ cup chopped onion
1 16-ounce can tomatoes, cut up
1 10-ounce package frozen whole kernel corn
1 cup thinly sliced carrot
½ cup chopped green pepper
1 4-ounce can mushroom stems and pieces, drained
2 tablespoons instant beef bouillon granules
1 teaspoon dried oregano, crushed

● In a 3-quart saucepan cook ground beef and onion till meat is browned and onion is tender. Drain off excess fat.

● Stir *undrained* tomatoes, corn, carrot, green pepper, mushrooms, bouillon granules, oregano, 3 cups *water*, and dash *pepper* into the cooked meat mixture. Bring to boiling; reduce heat. Cover and simmer about 15 minutes or till vegetables are tender, stirring occasionally. Makes 5 servings.

**Chutney-Turkey
Salad Sandwiches**

Chutney-Turkey Salad Sandwiches

Since you'll only use half of the buns in this recipe, freeze the rest for another time.

1½ cups finely chopped cooked
  turkey *or* chicken
⅓ cup mayonnaise *or* salad
  dressing
¼ cup chutney
2 tablespoons finely chopped
  sweet red *or* green pepper
1 to 1½ teaspoons curry
  powder
1 13¾-ounce package hot roll
  mix
1 beaten egg white
¼ cup finely chopped peanuts
  Leaf lettuce

● For filling, combine cooked turkey or chicken, mayonnaise or salad dressing, chutney, chopped pepper, and curry powder. Cover and chill for several hours.

● Meanwhile, to make the buns, prepare the hot roll mix according to package directions. Shape dough into 12 balls. Press balls flat between hands. Place on a greased baking sheet; press into 3-inch circles.

● Brush tops of buns with beaten egg white; sprinkle with finely chopped peanuts, pressing peanuts lightly into buns.

● Cover buns; let rise in a warm place till nearly double (about 30 minutes). Bake in a 375° oven for 15 to 20 minutes or till golden brown. Cool on a wire rack.

● To serve, slice *6* of the cooled buns in half horizontally. Line the bottom half of each bun with lettuce. Spoon about ¼ cup filling onto each lettuce-lined bun; replace top halves of buns. Makes 6 servings.

Seafood Salad Sandwiches

Instead of a croissant, next time spread this moist filling on whole wheat bread or in a pita round.

1 4½-ounce can shrimp,
  rinsed and drained, *or* one
  6-ounce can crab meat,
  drained, flaked, and
  cartilage removed
1 small tomato, peeled,
  seeded, and finely
  chopped
½ cup shredded cheddar
  cheese
¼ cup finely chopped celery
3 tablespoons slivered
  almonds, toasted
1 tablespoon sliced green
  onion
¼ cup dairy sour cream
4 croissants
  Lettuce leaves

● Combine the canned shrimp or crab meat, chopped tomato, cheddar cheese, finely chopped celery, toasted almonds, and sliced green onion. Stir in sour cream. Cover and chill for several hours, if desired.

● To serve, slice the 4 croissants in half horizontally. Line the bottom half of each croissant with lettuce. Spoon about ⅓ cup of the shrimp mixture onto each lettuce-lined croissant; replace top halves of croissants. Makes 4 servings.

Tuna and Sprout Pockets

½ cup cream-style cottage
    cheese
¼ cup shredded mozzarella
    cheese
¼ cup shredded carrot
¼ cup plain yogurt
2 tablespoons mayonnaise *or*
    salad dressing
½ teaspoon dried marjoram *or*
    savory, crushed
1 6½-ounce can tuna (water
    pack), drained and broken
    into chunks
4 small pita bread rounds
2 tablespoons chopped
    pecans (optional)
1 cup fresh alfalfa sprouts

● Stir together cottage cheese, mozzarella cheese, shredded carrot, yogurt, mayonnaise or salad dressing, and crushed marjoram or savory. Fold in the tuna. Cover and chill for several hours, if desired.

● To serve, cut the pita bread rounds in half crosswise, forming 8 pockets. If desired, stir chopped pecans into the tuna mixture. Spoon about ¼ cup tuna mixture into each pita bread pocket. Place alfalfa sprouts in each pita pocket. Makes 4 servings.

Yes, You Can Dine Out and Eat Light

Meals away from home are no longer reserved only for special occasions. We often choose to dine out simply for convenience' sake or just for the fun of it! Away-from-home meals can fit within your light eating life-style if you consider what you eat.

● For a refreshing drink, try bottled mineral water with a slice of your favorite citrus fruit as a garnish. Or, if you're in the mood for wine, order a wine spritzer.

● Request that salad dressing be served *on the side* so you can control the portion added to your salad.

● Order appetizers (such as boiled shrimp or potato skins) with a salad for your main course.

● Choose a plain baked potato or another steamed or simmered vegetable instead of french fries. Skip sour cream and temper the amount of butter you use.

● Inquire about any low-calorie, low-fat, and/or low-salt items that the restaurant may have on its menu. More and more restaurants are expanding their menu choices to include these foods.

● Many of the major airlines also can serve you special low-calorie, low-fat, and/or low-salt meals if given advance notice; inquire about these items.

Cheese and Egg-Salad Crepewiches

Freeze unused crepes between layers of waxed paper, wrapped in moisture- and vaporproof-material, for up to 4 months. Thaw at room temperature 1 hour before using.

3 **hard-cooked eggs, chopped**
2 **tablespoons finely chopped celery**
2 **tablespoons finely chopped sweet pickle**
1 **green onion, thinly sliced**
1 **tablespoon chopped pimiento**
2 **tablespoons mayonnaise** *or* **salad dressing**
2 **tablespoons shredded cheddar** *or* **American cheese**
1½ **teaspoons Dijon-style mustard**
Dash salt
10 **Basic Crepes**
Lettuce leaves

● For filling, combine hard-cooked eggs, celery, sweet pickle, green onion, and pimiento. Stir together mayonnaise, shredded cheese, mustard, and salt; toss with egg mixture. Cover; chill.

● Meanwhile, prepare Basic Crepes. To assemble crepewiches fold 1 crepe in half, forming a semicircle. (Put the *unbrowned* side of the crepe on the inside.) Place a lettuce leaf on crepe, positioning lettuce so it extends beyond rounded edge of crepe.

● Bring the corners of the crepe together and overlap, forming a cone; secure with a toothpick. Fill folded crepe with about 2 slightly rounded tablespoons of the filling. Repeat with the remaining 9 crepes and filling. Makes 5 servings.

Basic Crepes: Combine 2 *eggs*, 1½ cups *milk*, 1 cup all-purpose *flour*, 1 tablespoon *cooking oil*, and ¼ teaspoon *salt*. Beat with a rotary beater till blended. Heat a lightly greased 6-inch skillet. Remove from heat. Spoon in about 2 tablespoons batter; lift and tilt skillet to spread batter. Return to heat; brown on one side only. Invert pan over paper towel; remove crepe. Repeat to make 18 to 20 crepes, greasing skillet occasionally.

Making "crepewiches"
While the filling is chilling, prepare the crepes following the directions above. Freeze all but ten crepes.

Fold each crepe in half so it forms a semicircle. Fold crepes so the attractive, lightly browned side is on the outside. Place a lettuce leaf on each semicircle so the leaf is flush with the straight edge of the crepe, but extends slightly beyond the rounded edge. (You may have to fold or tear your lettuce leaves in half.)

Bring the corners of each crepe together and overlap them to form a cone, as shown. Secure with a toothpick. Carefully spoon filling into each crepe.

Mix-and-Match Sandwiches

¼ cup mayonnaise *or* salad
    dressing
¼ cup plain yogurt
1½ teaspoons minced dried
    onion
1 teaspoon prepared
    horseradish
1 teaspoon prepared mustard
    Dash garlic powder
2 brown-and-serve French
    rolls
4 lettuce leaves
6 ounces thinly sliced cooked
    lean beef, pork, chicken,
    turkey, *or* ham
4 ounces sliced cheddar,
    Swiss, American, *or*
    mozzarella cheese
    Thinly sliced tomatoes,
    thinly sliced cucumbers,
    or bean sprouts

● In a small bowl stir together mayonnaise or salad dressing, plain yogurt, minced dried onion, horseradish, mustard, and garlic powder. Let stand for 10 minutes to rehydrate the dried onion and blend the flavors.

● Meanwhile, bake the brown-and-serve French rolls according to package directions; cool.

● To serve, slice French rolls in half horizontally. Spread about *1 tablespoon* of the mayonnaise mixture on the 4 roll halves. On each half arrange lettuce, desired meat, and desired sliced cheese. Top each with tomatoes, cucumbers, or bean sprouts. Spoon about *1 tablespoon* of the remaining mayonnaise mixture atop each sandwich. Makes 4 servings.

Beef-Vegetable Sandwiches

Try these easy-to-make sandwiches for a light, summertime evening meal.

½ cup plain yogurt
½ cup shredded carrot
1 tablespoon finely chopped
    onion
½ teaspoon dried basil *or*
    tarragon, crushed, *or*
    dried dillweed (optional)
4 croissants *or* 8 slices
    firm-textured whole
    wheat bread
    Lettuce leaves
1 large tomato, thinly sliced
8 ounces thinly sliced cooked
    lean beef
½ of a medium cucumber,
    thinly sliced
¼ cup shredded cheddar *or*
    American cheese
1 cup fresh alfalfa sprouts

● In a small bowl stir together the yogurt, shredded carrot, finely chopped onion, and basil, tarragon, or dillweed, if desired. Set mixture aside.

● To serve, slice the 4 croissants in half horizontally. Line the bottom half of each croissant with lettuce. Atop the lettuce, layer the tomato slices, beef, sliced cucumber, shredded cheese, and alfalfa sprouts.

● Spoon yogurt mixture atop each sandwich. Replace top halves of croissants. Makes 4 servings.

Tempting Side Dishes

We created these vegetable and
salad recipes to blend with
your main course, not overpower
it. They're simple and versatile,
and positively intriguing.
You'll find yourself turning to
this chapter time and time again
for light-tasting
accompaniments to round out
your meals.

Vegetable Medley Stir-Fry

Toast sesame seeds by spreading a thin layer of the seeds in a shallow, ungreased pan. Heat in a 350° oven for 10 to 15 minutes, stirring once or twice. Store toasted seeds in the refrigerator.

1 cup fresh *or* frozen broccoli flowerets
1 cup fresh *or* frozen cauliflower flowerets
1 tablespoon olive *or* cooking oil
1 medium onion, cut into thin wedges
1 clove garlic, minced
1 small yellow crookneck squash *or* zucchini, halved lengthwise and sliced
1 tablespoon soy sauce *or* teriyaki sauce
1 teaspoon lemon pepper (optional)
½ teaspoon sesame oil
2 small tomatoes, cut into wedges
1 tablespoon sesame seed, toasted

● If using frozen broccoli or frozen cauliflower flowerets, place the frozen vegetables in a colander. Run hot water over the vegetables about 1 minute or till thawed. Drain well; set thawed vegetables aside.

● Preheat a wok or large skillet over medium-high heat; add the olive or cooking oil. Stir-fry onion and garlic in hot olive or cooking oil for 2 minutes; push to one side. Add fresh or thawed broccoli and cauliflower flowerets; stir-fry for 2 minutes or till crisp-tender; push aside. Add the crookneck squash or zucchini; stir-fry for 2 to 3 minutes more or till squash is crisp-tender. Stir in soy sauce or teriyaki sauce, lemon pepper, and sesame oil; add tomato wedges. Cover and cook over low heat about 1 minute more or till heated through.

● Turn vegetables into a serving bowl. Sprinkle with toasted sesame seed. Makes 6 servings.

Marinated Brussels Sprouts

If buying fresh brussels sprouts, choose those that are small and compact, with vivid green color.

1 pound brussels sprouts *or* two 10-ounce packages frozen brussels sprouts
½ cup vinegar
¼ cup salad oil
1 clove garlic, minced
3 tablespoons sliced green onion
1 tablespoon snipped fresh dill *or* 1 teaspoon dried dillweed
2 teaspoons honey
½ teaspoon salt
⅛ teaspoon pepper

● If using fresh brussels sprouts, trim the stems slightly. Remove the wilted or discolored leaves and wash. Cut sprouts in half lengthwise. Cook sprouts, covered, in a small amount of boiling salted water about 5 minutes or till crisp-tender. Drain well. (*Or,* if using frozen brussels sprouts, cook whole sprouts according to package directions. Drain and halve sprouts.) Cool cooked sprouts.

● For the marinade, in a bowl stir together the vinegar, salad oil, garlic, green onion, fresh dill or dried dillweed, honey, salt, and pepper. Gently stir in the drained and cooled brussels sprouts.

● Cover the bowl; marinate in the refrigerator for several hours or overnight, stirring occasionally. Drain brussels sprouts before serving. Makes 6 servings.

Vegetable Medley Stir-Fry

Italian-Style Eggplant Slices

A crisp, bread crumb coating complements the soft texture of the baked eggplant.

1 small eggplant, cut into
   ½-inch slices (about 12
   ounces)
½ cup creamy Italian *or*
   creamy cucumber salad
   dressing
¾ cup fine dry bread crumbs
1 large tomato, very thinly
   sliced
⅓ cup shredded mozzarella *or*
   Monterey Jack cheese

● Dip eggplant slices into creamy Italian or creamy cucumber salad dressing, then into bread crumbs to coat.

● Place the eggplant slices in an ungreased 15x10x1-inch baking pan. Bake in a 350° oven for 25 to 30 minutes or till eggplant is tender.

● Top *each* eggplant slice with a thin tomato slice and shredded mozzarella or Monterey Jack cheese. Bake about 2 minutes more or till cheese melts. Makes 5 servings.

Chilled Sesame Broccoli

Look for sesame oil, with its concentrated nutlike flavor, in supermarkets or Oriental food shops.

1 pound broccoli, cut into
   spears, *or* one 10-ounce
   package frozen broccoli
   spears
2 tablespoons vinegar
1 tablespoon soy sauce
1 teaspoon sugar
¼ teaspoon sesame oil
1 tablespoon sesame seed,
   toasted

● If using fresh broccoli, cut off broccoli flowerets; set aside. Bias-slice the broccoli stems into ½-inch-thick pieces. Cook stems, covered, in 1 inch of boiling salted water for 5 minutes; add reserved broccoli flowerets. Cook about 5 minutes more or till crisp-tender. Drain well. (*Or,* if using frozen broccoli cook spears according to package directions, *except* cook for only *half* of the suggested time. Drain the cooked broccoli. Cut off flowerets; bias-slice stems into ½-inch-thick pieces.) Cover and chill cooked broccoli.

● In a screw-top jar combine vinegar, soy sauce, sugar, and sesame oil. Cover and shake well to mix.

● Shake vinegar mixture again just before serving. Drizzle over chilled broccoli; toss gently. Sprinkle with toasted sesame seed. Makes 4 servings.

Ginger-Marinated Vegetables

For an attractive presentation, serve this deli-like side dish on individual lettuce-lined plates.

⅓ cup lemon juice
3 tablespoons water
3 tablespoons olive *or* salad oil
2 teaspoons snipped chives
2 teaspoons honey
1½ teaspoons grated gingerroot
¼ teaspoon salt
1 9-ounce package frozen artichoke hearts, thawed and cut in half
1 cup frozen crinkle-cut carrots, thawed
1 cup frozen peas, thawed
½ cup frozen small whole onions, thawed
½ cup cherry tomatoes, halved

● For the marinade, in a screw-top jar combine lemon juice, water, olive or salad oil, chives, honey, gingerroot, and salt. Cover and shake well to mix. Set aside.

● In a bowl combine thawed and halved artichoke hearts, thawed carrots, thawed peas, thawed onions, and cherry tomato halves. Stir in the marinade.

● Cover and marinate in the refrigerator for several hours or overnight, stirring occasionally. Drain vegetables before serving. Makes 6 servings.

Green Beans in Hot Vinaigrette

Vinaigrette (vin uh GRET) is a thin vinegar and oil mixture used to dress or marinate vegetables, salads, meats, or fish.

¾ pound green beans *or* one 9-ounce package frozen whole green beans
⅓ cup chopped green onion
2 cloves garlic, minced
2 tablespoons snipped parsley
1 tablespoon red wine vinegar
1 teaspoon Dijon-style mustard
1 tablespoon olive *or* cooking oil
Dash salt
Dash pepper

● Wash fresh green beans; remove ends and strings. In a saucepan cook fresh whole green beans, green onion, and garlic, covered, in a small amount of boiling salted water for 5 to 6 minutes or till crisp-tender. (*Or,* cook frozen green beans with onion and garlic according to package directions.) Drain vegetables well; return to saucepan.

● For vinaigrette dressing, in a small mixing bowl combine parsley, red wine vinegar, and mustard. Gradually add olive or cooking oil, stirring constantly with a whisk or fork. Add the salt and pepper; stir till well mixed.

● Pour dressing over vegetables in saucepan. Cook about 1 minute or till heated through. Makes 4 servings.

Lemon Asparagus and Carrots

If you can't find the "baby" carrots, cut medium carrots into shorter lengths.

½ **pound asparagus *or* one
 8-ounce package frozen
 asparagus spears**
½ **pound small carrots
 Lemon juice
 Lemon pepper
 Lemon wedges (optional)
 Snipped parsley (optional)**

● To prepare fresh asparagus, wash and scrape off scales. Snap off and discard the woody bases. Tie the whole asparagus spears in a bundle. Stand the bundle upright in a deep kettle, letting tips extend 2 to 3 inches above boiling salted water. Cover and cook for 10 to 15 minutes or till crisp-tender. (*Or*, cook frozen asparagus spears according to package directions.) Rinse the cooked asparagus spears in cold water; drain.

● Meanwhile, to prepare carrots, wash, trim, and peel the small carrots. Place the carrots in a steamer basket above boiling water. Cover and steam about 15 minutes or till crisp-tender. Rinse the cooked carrots in cold water; drain.

● Cover and chill the cooked and drained asparagus spears and carrots. To serve, arrange the asparagus spears and carrots on a serving platter. Sprinkle with a little lemon juice and lemon pepper. Garnish with lemon wedges and parsley, if desired. Makes 6 servings.

Buying and Storing Fresh Asparagus

You'll be able to find fresh asparagus in most markets from mid-February through June. Choose firm, straight stalks with tight, compact tips. Asparagus with wilted stalks or loose tips may be tough and rather stringy.

Wrap the stem ends of the asparagus in moist paper towels before refrigerating in a plastic bag or covered container. Use fresh asparagus within two days.

1 Cooking fresh asparagus spears

Begin preparing asparagus spears by rinsing them and gently scraping off the scales with a knife. Remove the woody bases by breaking stalks instead of cutting them. Stalks will snap easily where tender part begins.

Tie the asparagus stalks together in a bundle. Stand the bundle upright in a deep kettle of boiling salted water. Let tips extend 2 to 3 inches above boiling water to avoid overcooking. (*Or,* cook in a saucepan in a small amount of boiling salted water with tips propped up out of the water with crumpled foil.) Cover and cook for 10 to 15 minutes or till crisp-tender.

2 Steaming carrots

Before steaming, wash, trim, and peel the small carrots. (*Or,* if you need to use medium carrots, cut them into 3- to 4-inch lengths.)

Place the carrots in a steamer basket. The steamer basket will allow the carrots to steam without coming in contact with the boiling liquid.

Place the basket of carrots over (but not touching) boiling water in a saucepan. Cover the pan and steam the carrots about 15 minutes or till crisp-tender.

New Potatoes Dijon

New potatoes are small, immature potatoes and not a specific variety.

1 pound tiny new potatoes *or* medium potatoes
¼ cup tarragon vinegar *or* vinegar
3 tablespoons olive *or* cooking oil
1 tablespoon Dijon-style mustard
¼ teaspoon salt
¼ teaspoon dried basil, crushed
⅛ teaspoon pepper
1 cup torn fresh spinach

● Scrub the potatoes. Remove a narrow strip of peel from the center of each new potato or quarter each medium potato.

● Cook potatoes, covered, in boiling salted water till tender (allow 10 to 15 minutes for new potatoes; 20 to 25 minutes for quartered medium potatoes). Drain well.

● For dressing, in a screw-top jar combine vinegar, olive or cooking oil, mustard, salt, dried basil, and pepper. Cover and shake well to mix. Pour dressing over the cooked and drained potatoes. Cover potato mixture; chill for several hours, stirring occasionally.

● To serve, add torn fresh spinach to potato mixture. Toss lightly. Serve immediately. Makes 6 servings.

Sectioning Citrus Fruits

To section grapefruit or oranges, begin by cutting off the peel and the white membrane. Work on a cutting board and cut down from the top of the fruit. (If desired, first cut a thin slice from one end of the fruit so it will sit level on the cutting board.) You'll need a sharp utility knife or a serrated knife for peeling citrus fruits.

Next, remove the sections by cutting into the center of the fruit between one section and the membrane. Then turn the knife and slide the knife down the other side of the section next to the membrane. Remove any seeds.

Citrus-Marinated Salad

If you score the peel of the cucumber by running the tines of a fork down the peel before slicing, you'll get attractive slices that are tender to eat.

2 oranges
1 grapefruit
1 avocado, seeded, peeled, and sliced
½ of a small cucumber, scored and thinly sliced
½ of a small onion, thinly sliced and separated into rings
Orange juice
¼ cup wine vinegar
1 tablespoon sugar
Dash salt
Dash pepper
Lettuce leaves

● Peel the oranges and the grapefruit. Section the oranges and the grapefruit over a small bowl so you catch the fruit juices; reserve juices.
● In a large bowl combine the orange and grapefruit sections, avocado slices, cucumber slices, and onion rings; set aside.
● For the marinade, measure the reserved fruit juices; add enough orange juice to make ⅓ cup. Combine the juice mixture, vinegar, sugar, salt, and pepper. Pour over fruit mixture; toss gently. Cover and marinate in the refrigerator for several hours, stirring occasionally.
● Before serving, use a slotted spoon to remove fruit mixture from marinade. Arrange fruit mixture on lettuce-lined plates. Drizzle marinade over each salad. Makes 4 servings.

Sunflower-Strawberry Salad

Try strawberry, peach, or another flavor of yogurt to vary the taste slightly.

1 medium apple, cored and chopped
1 cup halved seedless green grapes
1 cup sliced strawberries
½ cup sliced celery
¼ cup raisins
½ cup lemon yogurt
2 tablespoons sunflower nuts
Lettuce leaves

● In a bowl combine chopped apple, halved grapes, sliced strawberries, sliced celery, and raisins; toss gently. Fold in the lemon yogurt. Cover and chill.
● Just before serving, stir in sunflower nuts. Serve on lettuce-lined plates. Makes 6 servings.

Fruit Slaw

Fruit Slaw

Orange yogurt replaces the traditional mayonnaise-style dressing usually found on slaw.

3 cups shredded cabbage
1 orange, peeled and
   sectioned
1 cup halved seedless
   red grapes
½ cup sliced celery
1 8-ounce carton orange
   yogurt
1 small apple, cored and
   chopped
¼ cup sunflower nuts
   (optional)
   Cabbage leaves

● In a large salad bowl combine shredded cabbage, orange sections, halved red grapes, and sliced celery.
● For dressing, combine the orange yogurt and chopped apple. Spread dressing over cabbage mixture. Cover; chill.
● Just before serving, gently toss salad; sprinkle with sunflower nuts, if desired. Serve on cabbage-lined plates. Makes 10 servings.

Spinach-Orange Toss

The piquant flavor of the blue cheese adds zip to this lightly flavored salad.

4 cups torn fresh spinach,
   lettuce, *or* romaine
½ teaspoon finely shredded
   orange peel (set aside)
2 oranges, peeled and
   sectioned
¾ cup sliced fresh mushrooms
⅓ cup crumbled blue cheese
3 tablespoons salad oil
1 tablespoon lemon juice
¼ teaspoon grated gingerroot
¼ cup slivered almonds,
   toasted

● For salad, in a large salad bowl place torn spinach, lettuce, or romaine. Add orange sections, sliced fresh mushrooms, and crumbled blue cheese. Toss lightly.
● For dressing, in a screw-top jar combine salad oil, lemon juice, gingerroot, and orange peel. Cover and shake well to mix.
● Pour dressing over salad. Toss lightly to coat. Sprinkle toasted almonds over salad. Serve immediately. Makes 6 servings.

Vermicelli Vinaigrette

If vermicelli isn't available, use spaghetti as a substitute.

2 ounces vermicelli, broken
1 6-ounce jar artichoke
    hearts, drained and halved
½ cup sliced fresh mushrooms
2 tablespoons salad oil
2 tablespoons red wine
    vinegar
1 clove garlic, minced
¼ teaspoon dried basil,
    crushed
⅛ teaspoon salt
    Dash pepper
1 medium tomato, peeled,
    seeded, and chopped
⅓ cup chopped walnuts,
    toasted
1 tablespoon snipped parsley
    Lettuce leaves (optional)

● Cook the broken vermicelli according to package directions; drain vermicelli well.

● For salad, combine cooked and drained vermicelli, halved artichoke hearts, and sliced mushrooms. Toss lightly.

● For vinaigrette dressing, in a screw-top jar combine the salad oil, red wine vinegar, minced garlic, dried basil, salt, and pepper. Cover and shake well to mix.

● Pour dressing over the salad; toss lightly. Cover and chill for several hours, stirring occasionally.

● Just before serving, add chopped tomato, walnuts, and parsley to salad. Toss lightly. Serve in a lettuce-lined bowl, if desired. Makes 4 servings.

Vegetable-Bulgur Pilaf

The colorful vegetables turn this pilaf into a striking meat accompaniment.

½ cup chopped onion
½ cup chopped celery
½ cup sliced fresh mushrooms
1 clove garlic, minced
1 tablespoon cooking oil
½ cup sliced carrots
½ cup sliced zucchini
½ cup chicken *or* beef broth
¼ cup sweet red *or* green
    pepper strips (optional)
¼ cup bulgur wheat
½ teaspoon dried
    tarragon, crushed
¼ teaspoon salt

● In a 2-quart saucepan cook chopped onion, chopped celery, sliced mushrooms, and garlic in hot oil about 5 minutes or till vegetables are tender but not brown.

● Stir in sliced carrots, sliced zucchini, chicken or beef broth, red or green pepper strips, bulgur, dried tarragon, and salt. Bring to boiling; reduce heat. Cover and simmer for 8 to 10 minutes or till vegetables are tender. Makes 4 servings.

Refreshing
and
Enticing
Desserts

Satisfy your sweet tooth by
splurging on one of our lightened
desserts—you'll find it to be a
gratifying finale! By highlighting
delicate custards, airy cakes,
and refreshing fruit combinations,
we're able to offer an assortment
of fresh-tasting desserts that
add a flavor boost to any meal.

Chocolate-Mint Cake Roll

If you have white crème de menthe, tint the cake filling with a few drops of green food coloring.

½ cup all-purpose flour
¼ cup unsweetened cocoa
    powder
 1 teaspoon baking powder
¼ teaspoon salt
 4 egg yolks
½ teaspoon vanilla
⅓ cup sugar
 4 egg whites
½ cup sugar
    Sifted powdered sugar
 1 cup whipping cream
 2 tablespoons green crème de
    menthe
    Chocolate Glaze

● Grease and lightly flour a 15x10x1-inch jelly roll pan; set aside. Stir together flour, cocoa powder, baking powder, and salt; set aside.

● In a small mixer bowl beat egg yolks and vanilla with an electric mixer on high speed about 5 minutes or till thick and lemon colored. Gradually add the ⅓ cup sugar, beating till sugar dissolves. Thoroughly wash beaters.

● In a large mixer bowl beat egg whites with an electric mixer on medium speed till soft peaks form (tips curl). Gradually add the ½ cup sugar, beating till stiff peaks form (tips stand straight). Fold egg yolk mixture into beaten egg whites. Sprinkle flour mixture over egg mixture; fold in gently.

● Spread batter evenly in prepared pan. Bake in a 375° oven for 12 to 15 minutes or till a wooden toothpick inserted in center comes out clean.

● Immediately loosen edges of cake from pan and turn cake out onto a towel sprinkled with sifted powdered sugar. Starting with a narrow end, carefully roll the warm cake and towel up together. Cool cake, seam side down, on a wire rack.

● Meanwhile, for filling, beat cream till soft peaks form; fold in crème de menthe. Unroll cake; spread the filling to within 1 inch of the edges. Roll up cake and filling. Pour Chocolate Glaze over top of cake roll, allowing it to drizzle down sides. Chill cake roll thoroughly. Makes 12 servings.

Chocolate Glaze: In a small saucepan combine ¼ cup *sugar* and 2 teaspoons *cornstarch*. Stir in ⅓ cup *water;* add ½ square (½ ounce) *unsweetened chocolate*, cut up. Cook and stir till the chocolate is melted and mixture is thickened and bubbly. Cook and stir 2 minutes more. Remove saucepan from heat; stir in ½ teaspoon *vanilla.*

Chocolate-Mint Cake Roll

Pineapple-Coconut Cream Puffs

2 tablespoons sugar
2 teaspoons cornstarch
1 8-ounce can crushed
   pineapple (juice pack)
2 teaspoons lemon juice
2 beaten egg yolks
¼ cup coconut
2 egg whites
⅛ teaspoon cream of tartar
   Cream Puffs

● For filling, in a saucepan combine sugar and cornstarch. Stir in *undrained* pineapple and lemon juice. Cook and stir till thickened and bubbly. Cook and stir for 2 minutes more. Remove from heat.

● Gradually stir about *1 cup* of the hot pineapple mixture into the beaten egg yolks. Return mixture to saucepan. Cook and stir for 2 minutes more. Pour into a bowl; stir in coconut. Cover surface with clear plastic wrap or waxed paper; cool well.

● In a mixer bowl beat egg whites and cream of tartar till stiff peaks form (tips stand straight). Gently fold in the cooled pineapple mixture. Chill thoroughly.

● Prepare Cream Puffs. Set aside to cool.

● Just before serving, fill each cream puff with about ⅓ cup of the filling. Makes 8 servings.

Cream Puffs: In a saucepan bring ½ cup *water* and 2 tablespoons *butter or margarine* to boiling. Add ½ cup all-purpose *flour* and ⅛ teaspoon *salt* all at once; stir vigorously. Cook and stir till mixture forms a ball that doesn't separate. Remove from heat; cool 10 minutes. Add 2 *eggs,* 1 at a time, beating about 30 seconds after each addition or till smooth.

● Drop mixture by heaping tablespoonfuls into 8 portions, 3 inches apart, on a lightly greased baking sheet. Bake in a 400° oven about 30 minutes or till golden brown and puffy. Remove from oven; cut off tops. Use a fork to remove the soft center from each puff.

Lime Mousse

1 envelope unflavored gelatin
1 6-ounce can frozen limeade
   concentrate, thawed
¼ cup cold water
5 *or* 6 drops green food
   coloring (optional)
4 slightly beaten egg yolks
4 egg whites
1 8-ounce container frozen
   whipped dessert topping,
   thawed
   Lime slices (optional)

● In a small saucepan soften gelatin in limeade concentrate and water for 5 minutes. Stir in food coloring, if desired. Heat and stir till gelatin is dissolved and mixture is very hot.

● Gradually stir about *half* of the hot gelatin mixture into beaten egg yolks; return all to saucepan. Cook and stir till thickened and bubbly. Cook and stir for 2 minutes more. Remove from heat. Chill in ice water for 8 to 10 minutes or to the consistency of unbeaten egg whites (partially set), stirring frequently. Remove from ice water; set aside.

● Immediately beat egg whites till stiff peaks form (tips stand straight). Fold about ½ *cup* of the stiffly beaten egg whites into the gelatin mixture. Fold gelatin mixture into remaining egg whites. Fold in thawed dessert topping.

● Transfer mixture to a 1½-quart soufflé dish. Cover and chill about 6 hours or overnight. Garnish with lime slices, if desired. Makes 8 servings.

Raspberry Soufflé

Every bite of this exceptionally airy soufflé will melt in your mouth!

2 cups frozen red raspberries (lightly sweetened), thawed
1 envelope unflavored gelatin
½ cup cold water
2 slightly beaten egg yolks
1 tablespoon lemon juice
½ teaspoon vanilla
3 egg whites
¼ cup sugar
½ cup evaporated skimmed milk, chilled

● Attach a waxed paper or foil collar to a 1½-quart soufflé dish (see photograph, page 34). Set dish aside. Place a small mixer bowl and beaters in freezer.

● Put raspberries into a blender container or food processor bowl. Cover; blend till smooth. Pour berries into a sieve; press berries through sieve with a spoon to remove seeds. Set sieved raspberry pulp and juice aside (you should have about ¾ cup).

● In a saucepan soften gelatin in water for 5 minutes. Add egg yolks; cook and stir over low heat till gelatin dissolves and mixture coats a metal spoon. Stir in lemon juice and vanilla. Cool slightly. Stir in sieved raspberries. Chill till slightly thickened.

● Beat egg whites with an electric mixer till soft peaks form (tips curl). Gradually add sugar, beating till stiff peaks form (tips stand straight). Fold beaten egg whites into chilled gelatin-raspberry mixture.

● Using the chilled bowl and beaters, beat the chilled evaporated skimmed milk till stiff peaks form (tips stand straight); fold into gelatin-raspberry mixture.

● Transfer mixture to prepared 1½-quart soufflé dish. Chill about 6 hours or till firm. Peel off collar. Makes 10 servings.

Sieving raspberries

For a soufflé with a really smooth texture, you'll have to sieve the raspberries to remove the seeds.

To sieve the berries, place a sieve over a bowl. Pour the raspberries out of the blender container or food processor bowl into the sieve.

Work the fruit through the sieve with the back of a wooden spoon. Discard the raspberry seeds that remain in the sieve.

Orange-Strawberry Sponge Cake

Orange-Strawberry Sponge Cake

After beating the egg yolks, remember to wash the beaters well before using them to beat the egg whites. Any trace of fat left from the yolks will prevent the whites from whipping properly.

1¼ cups all-purpose flour
⅓ cup sugar
6 egg yolks
4 teaspoons finely shredded orange peel
½ cup orange juice
⅔ cup sugar
¼ teaspoon salt
6 egg whites
1 teaspoon cream of tartar
½ cup sugar
½ cup strawberry preserves
1 4-ounce container frozen whipped dessert topping, thawed
2 cups strawberries, sliced
1 cup strawberries, halved
Orange peel, cut into thin strips (optional)

● Combine flour and the ⅓ cup sugar; set aside. In a small mixer bowl beat egg yolks with an electric mixer on high speed about 5 minutes or till thick and lemon colored.

● Combine *3 teaspoons* of the shredded orange peel and the orange juice; add to beaten eggs yolks, beating on low speed till combined. Gradually add the ⅔ cup sugar and salt, beating on medium speed till sugar dissolves. Gradually add about ¼ of the flour mixture to yolk mixture, beating on low speed till combined. Repeat with remaining flour mixture, ¼ at a time, beating a total of about 2 minutes.

● Thoroughly wash beaters. In a large mixer bowl beat egg whites and cream of tartar on medium speed till soft peaks form (tips curl). Gradually add the ½ cup sugar, beating till stiff peaks form (tips stand straight). Stir about *1 cup* of the beaten egg whites into the egg yolk mixture. By hand, fold yolk mixture into remaining egg whites.

● Transfer mixture to an *ungreased* 10-inch tube pan. Bake in a 325° oven about 1 hour or till cake springs back and leaves no imprint when lightly touched. Invert cake in pan; cool completely. Loosen from pan; remove.

● In a small saucepan heat the strawberry preserves and the remaining 1 teaspoon shredded orange peel just till melted. To assemble cake, carefully cut the cake into 3 horizontal layers. Spread ⅓ of the whipped dessert topping over the bottom layer of cake. Arrange *1 cup* of sliced strawberries atop dessert topping; drizzle with ⅓ of the melted preserves. Top with another cake layer. Spread another ⅓ of whipped dessert topping over cake. Arrange remaining 1 cup sliced strawberries atop; drizzle with another ⅓ of preserves. Top with remaining cake layer. Spread remaining whipped topping over cake. Top with the 1 cup halved strawberries; drizzle with the remaining preserves.

● Garnish cake with thin strips of orange peel, if desired. Makes 12 servings.

Chocolate-Almond Custards

Dress up these individual baked custards by topping them with toasted almonds.

2 cups milk
½ of a 6-ounce package (½ cup) semisweet chocolate pieces
3 slightly beaten eggs
¼ cup sugar
¼ teaspoon almond extract

● In a small saucepan combine milk and chocolate pieces. Cook and stir over low heat till chocolate melts.
● Combine eggs, sugar, and almond extract; gradually add chocolate mixture, beating with an electric mixer on low speed or a rotary beater just till smooth.
● Place six 6-ounce custard cups in a 13x9x2-inch baking pan; set pan on an oven rack. Divide the chocolate mixture among the 6 custard cups.
● Pour boiling water into baking pan around custard cups to a depth of 1 inch. Bake in a 325° oven for 40 to 45 minutes or till a knife inserted near centers comes out clean.
● Serve custards warm or chilled. Makes 6 servings.

Rhubarb-Banana Bread Pudding

We've added new twists to the classic bread pudding—fruit in the bread layer and a golden meringue for a topping.

1 cup chopped fresh *or* frozen rhubarb
1½ cups apricot nectar
1 small banana, sliced
2 beaten egg yolks
2 tablespoons sugar
½ teaspoon ground cinnamon
½ teaspoon vanilla
2½ cups dry bread cubes (3½ slices)
2 egg whites
¼ teaspoon cream of tartar
2 tablespoons sugar

● Thaw rhubarb, if frozen. Combine fresh or thawed rhubarb, apricot nectar, banana, egg yolks, 2 tablespoons sugar, cinnamon, and vanilla. Stir in dry bread cubes.
● Transfer rhubarb mixture to an 8x1½-inch round baking dish. Bake in a 350° oven about 20 minutes.
● For meringue, beat egg whites and cream of tartar with an electric mixer on medium speed till soft peaks form (tips curl). Gradually add 2 tablespoons sugar, beating till stiff peaks form (tips stand straight).
● Dollop the meringue around the sides of the hot rhubarb mixture. Bake for 10 to 12 minutes more or till meringue is golden. Makes 6 servings.

Strawberry-Rice Fluff

Serve this '80s version of rice pudding as the climax to a special meal.

1 cup light cream
½ cup milk
¼ cup long grain rice
2 tablespoons sugar
1 teaspoon finely shredded
    orange peel
½ teaspoon vanilla
1 teaspoon unflavored gelatin
1 tablespoon cold water
1 pint strawberries
2 egg whites
¼ cup sugar

● In a heavy saucepan combine cream and milk; bring to boiling. Stir in *uncooked* rice. Cover and cook over low heat for 25 to 30 minutes or till rice is tender and most of the liquid is absorbed, stirring occasionally. (Mixture may look curdled.) Remove from heat; stir in the 2 tablespoons sugar, orange peel, and vanilla.

● In a 1-cup measure soften the unflavored gelatin in the cold water for 5 minutes. Place the measuring cup in a saucepan of water; heat and stir till the gelatin dissolves. Stir into rice mixture. Cool thoroughly.

● Meanwhile, chop strawberries, reserving a few whole berries for garnish. Stir chopped berries into rice mixture.

● *Immediately* begin beating egg whites with an electric mixer on medium speed till soft peaks form (tips curl). Gradually add the ¼ cup sugar, beating till stiff peaks form (tips stand straight). Fold egg whites into rice mixture.

● Transfer rice mixture to 4 dessert dishes. Chill about 3 hours or overnight. Slice the reserved strawberries. Garnish each serving with sliced strawberries. Makes 4 servings.

**Folding in beaten
egg whites**
To fold the stiffly beaten egg whites into the rice mixture, cut down through the mixture with a rubber spatula. Scrape across the bottom of the saucepan, and bring the spatula up and over the rice mixture, close to the surface.

Repeat this circular down-up-and-over motion, turning the saucepan frequently for even distribution.

Do not *stir* the egg whites into the rice mixture. Stirring breaks down the fluffy consistency of the beaten egg whites.

Broiled Orange Boats

Refreshing as a dessert, these are just as good as part of your breakfast.

2 large oranges
1 cup seedless green *or* red
   grapes, halved
2 teaspoons sugar
¼ teaspoon ground cinnamon
2 tablespoons butter *or*
   margarine, melted
2 tablespoons coconut

● Halve oranges (use a sawtooth cut, if desired). Carefully remove fruit from each orange half, leaving shells intact. Section orange; cut fruit into chunks.
● Combine orange chunks, halved grapes, sugar, and cinnamon. Stir in the melted butter or margarine. Spoon fruit mixture into orange shells.
● Place the filled orange shells in a shallow baking pan. Sprinkle a little bit of coconut over fruit in each shell. Broil 5 to 6 inches from heat for 3 to 4 minutes or till the coconut is golden. Serve warm. Makes 4 servings.

Cutting a sawtooth edge
To make this decorative cut, insert a paring knife at a 45-degree angle through the peel in the middle of a whole orange. Push the knife all the way through to the center. Make the next cut at a 90-degree angle to the first, then push the knife through to the center of the orange. Continue making cuts around the middle of the orange until it is cut in half. Gently pull the orange apart to separate the halves.

Another way to cut a sawtooth edge around an orange is to use a "V-cutter" (pictured at lower left). You can purchase this specialty tool at kitchen supply stores.

Apples Poached in Sherry

The best cooking apples are firm varieties such as Rome Beauty, Granny Smith, and Jonathan.

4 medium cooking apples
⅔ cup apple juice *or* apple cider
¼ cup raisins
¼ cup dry sherry
3 inches stick cinnamon
1 teaspoon finely shredded lemon peel

● Core the apples. Peel off a strip around the top of each apple.

● In a medium skillet combine the apple juice or apple cider, raisins, dry sherry, stick cinnamon, and lemon peel.

● Bring sherry mixture to boiling. Add the apples to the skillet. Reduce heat; cover and simmer for 10 minutes, spooning the sherry mixture over apples occasionally. Turn apples over; cover and simmer for 3 to 5 minutes more or till tender. Remove the stick cinnamon.

● Serve apples warm. Spoon poaching liquid over apples, if desired. Makes 4 servings.

Fruity Floating Islands

For the freshest-tasting and best-looking poached meringues, serve your guests these delicacies the same day you make them.

3 egg whites
¼ teaspoon cream of tartar
¼ cup sugar
1¼ cups milk
3 slightly beaten egg yolks
2 tablespoons sugar
  Milk
½ teaspoon vanilla
  Dash ground nutmeg (optional)
3 cups desired fresh fruit*

● For meringue, beat egg whites and cream of tartar with an electric mixer on medium speed till soft peaks form (tips curl). Gradually add the ¼ cup sugar, beating till stiff peaks form (tips stand straight).

● In a heavy 10-inch skillet heat the 1¼ cups milk till hot but *not bubbling*. Drop meringue by spoonfuls into milk, making 6 mounds. Simmer, uncovered, about 5 minutes or till meringues are set. Lift meringues from milk with a slotted spoon. Drain meringues on paper towels (reserve milk in skillet for custard); chill the meringues well.

● Meanwhile, for the custard, in a medium saucepan combine the beaten egg yolks and the 2 tablespoons sugar. Measure the reserved milk; add enough additional milk to make 1½ cups. Stir milk into the yolk mixture.

● Cook and stir over low heat till mixture thickens slightly and coats a metal spoon. Remove from heat. Cool custard quickly by placing the saucepan in a sink or bowl of ice water and stirring for 1 to 2 minutes. Stir in vanilla and nutmeg, if desired.

● Spoon desired fresh fruit into 6 serving dishes. Spoon the custard over fruit. Top each serving with a chilled meringue. Makes 6 servings.

*Fruit Options: Choose one or any combination of the following: Peeled and sliced or cut-up bananas, kiwifruit, melon, papayas, or peaches; sliced or cut-up apricots, nectarines, or plums; peeled and sectioned oranges or tangerines; or berries (halve large strawberries).

Fruit Trifle

Instead of placing a special order for a bakery cake, prepare the sponge cake on page 77 and cut part of it into cubes.

<table>
<tr><td>2</td><td>eggs</td></tr>
<tr><td>1½</td><td>cups milk</td></tr>
<tr><td>¼</td><td>cup sugar</td></tr>
<tr><td>2</td><td>teaspoons finely shredded lemon peel</td></tr>
<tr><td>1</td><td>teaspoon vanilla</td></tr>
<tr><td>3</td><td>cups sliced strawberries, sliced bananas, and/or drained, canned pineapple chunks</td></tr>
<tr><td>2</td><td>tablespoons lemon juice</td></tr>
<tr><td>3</td><td>cups sponge cake or ladyfingers cut into ½-inch cubes</td></tr>
<tr><td>2</td><td>tablespoons dry sherry</td></tr>
<tr><td>2</td><td>tablespoons currant jelly</td></tr>
</table>

● For custard, in a saucepan lightly beat eggs. Stir in milk, sugar, and lemon peel. Cook and stir over medium heat for 10 to 12 minutes or till mixture thickens slightly and coats a metal spoon. Remove from heat. Cool custard quickly by placing the saucepan in a sink or bowl of ice water and stirring for 1 to 2 minutes. Stir in vanilla.

● If using bananas, toss the banana slices with the lemon juice to prevent browning (if not using bananas, omit the lemon juice). To assemble trifle, place *half* of the sponge cake or ladyfinger cubes in a 2½-quart soufflé dish or serving bowl. Sprinkle with *1 tablespoon* of the dry sherry; dot with the currant jelly. Layer the fruit atop the currant jelly. Top with the remaining sponge cake or ladyfinger cubes. Sprinkle with the remaining sherry. Spoon cooled custard over cake or ladyfinger cubes.

● Cover and refrigerate trifle about 6 hours. Makes 8 servings.

Baked Bananas

For a simpler presentation, remove all the peel from the bananas before serving this favorite Polynesian dessert.

<table>
<tr><td>4</td><td>firm medium bananas</td></tr>
<tr><td></td><td>Lime or lemon juice</td></tr>
<tr><td></td><td>Brown sugar</td></tr>
<tr><td></td><td>Finely chopped peanuts</td></tr>
</table>

● Place the *unpeeled* bananas in a shallow baking pan. Bake the bananas in a 325° oven for 20 to 25 minutes or till a fork will pierce the bananas easily.

● To serve, make 2 lengthwise slits, ½ to ¾ inch apart, through the peel of each banana. Remove the peel between the slits.

● Sprinkle each banana with a little lime or lemon juice and a little brown sugar. Top each banana with a few finely chopped peanuts. Makes 4 servings.

Watermelon Sorbet
(see recipe, page 84)

Cantaloupe Sorbet
(see recipe, page 84)

Honeydew Melon Sorbet
(see recipe, page 84)

Cantaloupe Sorbet

Sorbet (SOR-but) is French for sherbet. (Pictured on page 83.)

1 cup orange juice
¼ cup sugar
2 cups chopped cantaloupe
½ cup light cream
3 tablespoons lemon juice
2 egg whites
¼ cup sugar
Cantaloupe halves, chilled (optional)

● In a saucepan combine orange juice and ¼ cup sugar; bring to boiling, stirring occasionally to dissolve sugar. Reduce heat; simmer for 5 minutes. Cool.

● In a blender container or food processor bowl combine 2 cups chopped cantaloupe and light cream. Cover; blend or process about 1 minute or till smooth. Stir in the lemon juice and the cooled orange juice mixture. Transfer mixture to a 12x7½x2-inch baking dish or a 9x9x2-inch baking pan. Cover; freeze about 4 hours or till firm.

● Beat egg whites with an electric mixer on medium speed till soft peaks form (tips curl). Gradually add ¼ cup sugar, beating till stiff peaks form (tips stand straight). Break the frozen mixture into chunks; transfer mixture to a chilled mixer bowl. Beat frozen mixture with the electric mixer till smooth, but not melted. Fold in the beaten egg whites. Return to the 12x7½x2-inch baking dish. Cover; freeze sorbet for several hours or till firm.

● Let sorbet stand at room temperature about 5 minutes before serving. Serve sorbet on chilled cantaloupe halves, if desired. Makes 6 servings.

Honeydew Melon Sorbet: Prepare Cantaloupe Sorbet as above, *except* substitute chopped *honeydew melon* for the chopped cantaloupe. Stir in a few drops *green food coloring* with the lemon juice and cooled orange juice mixture, if desired. Serve on chilled *honeydew melon wedges,* if desired.

Watermelon Sorbet: Prepare Cantaloupe Sorbet as above, *except* substitute chopped *watermelon* for the chopped cantaloupe. Stir in a few drops *red food coloring* with the lemon juice and cooled orange juice mixture, if desired. Serve on chilled *watermelon slices,* if desired.

1 Beating a sorbet

After blending and freezing the fruit mixture, remove it from the freezer. Use a plastic or wooden spoon to break the mixture into chunks. The chunks should be small enough for easy mixing with an electric mixer.

Transfer the broken-up mixture to a large, chilled mixer bowl.

2

Begin beating the frozen chunks with an electric mixer on low speed. When the large chunks are broken up, continue beating with the electric mixer on high speed.

Beat till smooth, but do not allow the mixture to melt. Scrape down the sides of the bowl as necessary.

Fold in the beaten egg whites. The egg whites give the sorbet its fluffy and light texture.

Before serving, let the sorbet stand at room temperature about 5 minutes for easier scooping with an ice cream scoop.

Flaming Pears Caribbean

If you prefer a nonalcoholic dessert, omit the rum. Instead, stir 2 tablespoons water into the brown sugar mixture and skip the flaming step.

2 cups sliced, peeled fresh pears *or* one 16-ounce can pear slices, drained
1 tablespoon lime juice
¼ cup packed brown sugar
2 tablespoons butter *or* margarine
¼ cup rum
   Ground cinnamon
   Vanilla ice cream
   Seedless red grapes (optional)
   Lime wedges (optional)

● Toss the pear slices gently with the lime juice; set aside.
● In a medium skillet heat the brown sugar and butter or margarine till melted; stir in *half* of the rum. Stir in pear slices. Cook till pears are heated through, gently stirring the pear slices once. (Allow 3 to 4 minutes for the fresh pears; about 1 minute for the canned pears.) Transfer pear slices to a serving container; sprinkle generously with cinnamon.
● Pour the remaining rum into a small skillet or saucepan; heat over low heat just till hot. Remove from heat. Ignite rum and pour over pear slices.
● Serve pear slices over vanilla ice cream. Garnish with red grapes and lime wedges, if desired. Makes 6 servings.

Flaming desserts

When preparing flaming desserts, remember that although any liquor or liqueur is supposed to flame, best results will come from a recently opened bottle that is at least 70 proof. Liquor or liqueur from bottles that have been open for some time may be harder to flame and burn less brightly.

To flame this dessert, transfer the pear slices to a serving container and sprinkle with cinnamon. Pour the rum into a small skillet or saucepan. Heat over low heat just till hot; remove from heat. Quickly ignite the rum with a long match and carefully pour it over the pear slices.

Brandied Applesauce

Add a crunchy texture to the applesauce by sprinkling it with granola or toasted coconut.

2 pounds cooking apples, peeled, cored, and coarsely chopped
½ cup water
3 tablespoons brown sugar
¼ cup brandy

● In a heavy 3-quart saucepan combine the coarsely chopped apples, water, and brown sugar. Bring to boiling. Reduce heat; cover and simmer about 20 minutes or till desired consistency, mashing and stirring frequently with a potato masher. (Add more *water,* if necessary, to keep the applesauce from sticking to the saucepan.) Stir in the brandy and cook, covered, about 5 minutes more.
● Serve applesauce warm or chilled. Makes 5 servings.

Pineapple Frost

Fresh pineapple unavailable? Substitute a 20-ounce can of juice-pack crushed pineapple, draining and reserving ¾ cup of the juice to use in place of the canned juice.

1 small fresh pineapple
¾ cup sugar
2 cups light cream
1 6-ounce can (¾ cup) unsweetened pineapple juice
Few drops yellow food coloring (optional)

● To remove the crown from the fresh pineapple, hold the pineapple in one hand and the crown in the other; twist in opposite directions to separate. Peel the pineapple; remove eyes. Quarter and core pineapple. Chop pineapple into small pieces; measure 2 cups (refrigerate remainder for another use).
● Place chopped pineapple in a blender container or food processor bowl. Cover; blend or process till pureed. Transfer pureed pineapple to a mixing bowl; stir in sugar. Let mixture stand about 10 minutes or till sugar dissolves, stirring occasionally. Stir in light cream, unsweetened pineapple juice, and yellow food coloring, if desired.
● Transfer pineapple mixture to an 11x7x1½-inch baking pan. Cover and freeze overnight or till firm. Let stand at room temperature about 30 minutes before serving. Scoop into dessert bowls. Makes 6 servings.

Pinwheel Pears with
Raspberry Sauce

Pinwheel Pears with Raspberry Sauce

Use an apple corer or a pear corer to make quick work of cutting out the centers of the fresh pears.

1 3-ounce package cream
  cheese, softened
¼ cup ricotta cheese
2 tablespoons finely chopped
  pistachios *or* pecans
4 fresh medium pears
  Raspberry Sauce

● Combine the softened cream cheese, ricotta cheese, and pistachios or pecans; set aside.

● Wash pears; pat dry. Core each of the pears, leaving a center hole about 1 inch in diameter. Fill each pear with the cream cheese-nut mixture. Wrap the stuffed pears in clear plastic wrap or foil; chill till serving time.

● Just before serving, unwrap pears and cut crosswise into about ¼-inch-thick slices. Spoon a little of the Raspberry Sauce onto each serving plate. Arrange pear slices atop the Raspberry Sauce. Makes 6 servings.

Raspberry Sauce: Press 1½ cups fresh *red raspberries* through a sieve to remove the seeds. (*Or,* thaw 1½ cups frozen *red raspberries;* press through a sieve to remove the seeds.) In a small saucepan combine the sieved raspberry pulp and juice, 3 tablespoons *water,* 1 tablespoon *sugar,* and 1 teaspoon *cornstarch.* Cook and stir till thickened and bubbly. Cook and stir for 2 minutes more. Cover and chill.

Fruit Cup Slush

This palate refresher is full of fruit and topped with an icy slush.

1 16-ounce can unpeeled
  apricot halves (in
  extra-light syrup)
1½ cups ginger ale
1 teaspoon finely shredded
  orange peel
1 8-ounce can pineapple
  chunks (juice pack),
  drained
1 large banana, sliced
1 cup seedless green grapes
½ cup grapefruit sections

● For the slush, drain the apricot halves, reserving syrup. Combine the reserved apricot syrup, ginger ale, and orange peel. Pour mixture into an 8x4x2-inch loaf pan. Cover and freeze for 4 to 5 hours or just till mixture is slushy.

● In a bowl combine apricot halves, pineapple chunks, sliced banana, grapes, and grapefruit sections. Spoon fruit into 6 dessert dishes; top with slush. Makes 6 servings.

Nutrition Analysis

This nutrition analysis chart gives you the amount of calories, protein, carbohydrates, fats, sodium, and potassium in each serving of a recipe. The chart also gives the percentages of the United States Recommended Daily Allowances (USRDAs) for protein and certain vitamins and minerals per serving. Use the analyses to compare nutritional values of recipes. This information was obtained by a computerized method using Agriculture Handbook Number 456, published by the United States Department of Agriculture, as the primary source.

In compiling the nutrition analyses, we made the following assumptions:
● For the main-dish meat recipes, the nutrition analyses were calculated using measurements for cooked lean meat trimmed of fat.
● Garnishes and optional ingredients were not included in nutrition analyses.
● If a food was marinated and then brushed with marinade during cooking, the analysis includes the entire marinade amount.
● When two ingredient options appear in a recipe, calculations were made using the first choice.
● For ingredients of variable weight (such as "2½- to 3-pound broiler-fryer chicken"), calculations were made using the lesser weight.

	CALORIES	PROTEIN (g)	CARBOHYDRATE (g)	FAT (g)	SODIUM (mg)	POTASSIUM (mg)	PROTEIN	VITAMIN A	VITAMIN C	THIAMINE	RIBOFLAVIN	NIACIN	CALCIUM	IRON
	Per Serving						Percent USRDAs Per Serving							
Main Dishes														
Apples 'n' Cheddar Quiche (p. 36)	402	15	28	26	437	192	24	15	2	16	25	8	30	10
Beef-Vegetable Sandwiches (p. 58)	275	23	18	18	403	463	36	44	23	13	19	23	11	18
Broccoli-Ham Soup (p. 50)	299	20	15	18	828	495	31	29	74	29	26	16	19	13
Broiled Pork Chops and Vegetables (p. 13)	364	26	13	23	83	706	39	18	39	63	29	48	6	23
Broiled Vegetable Burgers (p. 9)	235	26	5	11	91	459	40	40	24	10	15	31	2	25
Cabbage-Tuna Toss (p. 43)	251	16	9	17	286	574	25	11	73	8	16	39	9	11
Cheese and Egg-Salad Crepewiches (p. 57)	224	10	16	13	241	246	15	17	17	11	17	5	11	10
Chicken-Avocado Salad (p. 40)	362	24	22	20	464	611	37	9	16	12	14	37	5	12
Chicken-Corn Chowder (p. 52)	284	22	25	11	580	613	34	7	25	13	18	33	11	9
Chicken Florentine (p. 18)	202	25	7	8	314	564	39	190	96	11	25	41	13	26
Chicken Pineapple Dijon (p. 19)	181	28	8	3	122	41	43	2	5	7	13	53	2	10
Chicken-Sesame Salad (p. 38)	229	24	5	13	210	451	36	11	12	7	12	32	4	11
Chicken, Shrimp, and Fruit Salad (p. 38)	297	21	28	12	146	642	32	24	34	6	9	26	5	13
Chilled Salmon Steaks with Dressing (p. 23)	263	38	4	16	185	618	58	81	4	17	19	26	11	6

	CALORIES	PROTEIN (g)	CARBOHYDRATE (g)	FAT (g)	SODIUM (mg)	POTASSIUM (mg)	PROTEIN	VITAMIN A	VITAMIN C	THIAMINE	RIBOFLAVIN	NIACIN	CALCIUM	IRON
	Per Serving						Percent USRDAs Per Serving							

Main Dishes *(continued)*

	CALORIES	PROTEIN (g)	CARBOHYDRATE (g)	FAT (g)	SODIUM (mg)	POTASSIUM (mg)	PROTEIN	VITAMIN A	VITAMIN C	THIAMINE	RIBOFLAVIN	NIACIN	CALCIUM	IRON
Chutney-Turkey Salad Sandwiches (p. 55)	350	17	32	17	312	302	26	6	13	14	11	24	3	9
Cinnamon Chicken Salad in Tomato Cups (p. 42)	331	24	14	21	331	737	37	27	54	15	13	35	7	13
Citrus-Glazed Chicken (p. 16)	236	24	11	10	48	111	37	23	15	10	30	37	3	15
Citrus-Marinated Fillets (p. 24)	144	17	10	4	198	142	26	.04	11	5	4	10	7	6
Classic Chef's Salad (p. 48)	288	27	8	16	450	620	42	31	84	16	25	20	34	19
Crustless Quiche Lorraine (p. 36)	241	14	5	18	277	185	22	18	3	8	19	2	26	9
Curried Fish Soup (p. 50)	175	19	9	7	595	416	30	32	6	4	11	19	10	4
Curried Salmon Salad (p. 42)	467	21	27	31	848	537	32	9	48	10	13	38	26	12
Easy Broiled Shrimp (p. 26)	226	30	13	6	873	538	46	4	67	7	5	26	11	17
Easy Oven-Fried Fish (p. 23)	197	21	15	6	270	574	32	3	31	16	10	14	9	9
Fruit and Lamb Kabobs (p. 11)	275	14	15	18	49	321	22	11	32	7	10	16	2	7
Grilled Steak with Italian Vegetables (p. 6)	186	17	9	9	76	637	26	29	109	11	15	23	5	15
Ground Beef and Vegetable Soup (p. 53)	280	20	21	14	750	647	31	86	71	13	17	29	3	20
Ham and Fruit Toss (p. 45)	234	16	26	8	453	545	25	11	74	27	19	11	25	13
Ham-Filled Omelets (p. 30)	329	27	3	23	656	341	41	30	11	22	31	12	20	22
Herbed Chicken à la Française (p. 20)	449	39	2	30	222	64	60	8	6	7	20	71	5	14
Lemony Lamb Chops (p. 12)	415	25	2	33	211	290	38	.03	6	9	15	28	1	8
Mexicali Oven-Fried Chicken (p. 18)	223	25	6	10	52	25	38	27	.06	8	30	37	2	15
Minestrone Soup (p. 53)	214	12	31	6	836	743	18	45	114	17	14	12	13	13
Mix-and-Match Sandwiches (p. 58)	401	23	20	25	495	343	36	15	16	12	20	17	26	16
Orange-Glazed Chicken (p. 19)	226	31	11	10	709	237	48	7	32	15	22	61	4	17
Oriental Beef and Vegetable Stir-Fry (p. 8)	355	22	42	10	1511	501	33	8	35	21	14	27	6	27
Pasta with Scallop and Wine Sauce (p. 26)	361	28	44	6	446	709	44	20	31	34	17	21	20	24
Pork Pinwheels with Apricot Stuffing (p. 13)	191	14	17	8	188	308	21	25	4	32	9	16	2	13
Puffy Vegetable Omelet (p. 28)	455	22	9	37	531	606	35	65	54	13	42	13	31	17
Seafood Salad Sandwich (p. 55)	278	15	16	23	417	245	23	13	14	9	14	9	19	12
Shrimp and Broccoli Quiche (p. 35)	423	23	27	25	486	366	35	31	38	16	25	12	40	14

Nutrition Analysis

	CALORIES	PROTEIN (g)	CARBOHYDRATE (g)	FAT (g)	SODIUM (mg)	POTASSIUM (mg)	PROTEIN	VITAMIN A	VITAMIN C	THIAMINE	RIBOFLAVIN	NIACIN	CALCIUM	IRON
	Per Serving						Percent USRDAs Per Serving							
Main Dishes *(continued)*														
Shrimp Salad (p. 45)	289	23	17	15	138	507	35	102	99	10	7	11	18	22
Spicy Beef Salad (p. 46)	243	19	4	17	159	327	30	23	16	6	15	13	18	14
Spinach-Mushroom Soufflé Roll (p. 33)	515	22	23	38	798	620	34	153	37	20	44	9	36	22
Spinach, Shrimp, and Cheese Soufflé (p. 34)	364	23	11	24	387	293	36	51	12	10	25	6	29	18
Stuffed Flank Steak Teriyaki (p. 6)	305	22	22	14	1814	394	34	22	5	8	14	19	6	26
Sweet and Sour Pork (p. 14)	295	15	29	13	529	326	23	28	35	21	9	14	3	14
Tabouleh-Seafood Salad (p. 46)	519	25	72	16	524	598	38	12	104	22	18	35	10	38
Taco Salad (p. 47)	512	29	44	26	875	688	44	60	118	18	31	34	32	30
Tuna and Sprout Pockets (p. 56)	252	23	18	9	169	203	35	20	1	9	12	34	12	10
Turkey and Rice Soup (p. 52)	339	24	30	14	866	604	37	27	59	23	24	34	18	14
Veal Loaf (p. 14)	263	25	9	13	494	296	39	27	6	9	21	27	7	19
Vegetable-Cheese Soufflé (p. 33)	435	21	17	32	609	441	32	96	11	13	31	4	35	15
Wine-Poached Fish with Vegetable Sauce (p. 25)	229	25	5	10	264	710	38	50	4	7	10	52	3	7
Side Dishes														
Chilled Sesame Broccoli (p. 62)	58	5	9	2	348	372	7	57	214	8	16	6	12	9
Citrus-Marinated Salad (p. 67)	169	3	22	10	7	622	4	9	106	11	10	7	5	7
Fruit Slaw (p. 69)	44	1	9	1	24	177	2	2	37	3	4	1	5	2
Ginger-Marinated Vegetables (p. 63)	115	3	13	7	62	273	5	62	33	9	7	6	3	5
Green Beans in Hot Vinaigrette (p. 63)	54	1	5	4	19	152	2	14	19	4	4	2	4	4
Italian-Style Eggplant Slices (p. 62)	228	4	17	16	631	193	7	6	13	7	6	6	7	6

	CALORIES	PROTEIN (g)	CARBOHYDRATE (g)	FAT (g)	SODIUM (mg)	POTASSIUM (mg)	PROTEIN	VITAMIN A	VITAMIN C	THIAMINE	RIBOFLAVIN	NIACIN	CALCIUM	IRON
	Per serving						Percent USRDAs Per Serving							
Lemon Asparagus and Carrots (p. 64)	26	1	6	0	19	238	2	90	28	6	6	4	2	4
Marinated Brussels Sprouts (p. 60)	127	4	10	9	189	326	6	10	130	5	7	4	3	7
New Potatoes Dijon (p. 66)	109	2	11	7	130	287	3	15	27	4	2	5	2	4
Spinach-Orange Toss (p. 69)	149	4	8	12	80	334	7	63	67	6	13	5	9	10
Sunflower-Strawberry Salad (p. 67)	102	2	21	2	29	301	4	3	34	8	5	3	6	6
Vegetable-Bulgur Pilaf (p. 70)	103	4	15	4	365	294	5	42	27	5	6	8	3	6
Vegetable Medley Stir-Fry (p. 60)	58	2	6	4	227	254	3	14	66	4	5	4	3	4
Vermicelli Vinaigrette (p. 70)	199	5	18	14	93	305	8	8	20	14	11	10	3	7
Desserts														
Apples Poached In Sherry (p. 81)	139	1	33	1	5	277	1	3	11	4	3	1	2	6
Baked Bananas (p. 82)	154	3	34	2	4	498	4	5	21	5	5	8	2	6
Brandied Applesauce (p. 87)	108	0	21	1	4	126	0	2	6	2	1	1	1	3
Broiled Orange Boats (p. 80)	140	1	21	7	72	242	2	9	90	7	3	2	4	3
Cantaloupe Sorbet (p. 84)	149	3	26	4	32	267	4	41	70	5	5	3	3	2
Chocolate-Almond Custards (p. 78)	198	7	21	11	93	196	10	8	1	3	13	1	11	5
Chocolate-Mint Cake Roll (p. 72)	195	4	26	9	99	86	6	9	0	4	7	2	4	4
Flaming Pears Caribbean (p. 86)	243	3	35	9	80	258	4	7	9	3	8	1	8	4
Fruit Cup Slush (p. 89)	144	1	37	0	2	372	2	30	26	5	3	3	2	4
Fruit Trifle (p. 82)	213	6	38	5	81	247	9	8	30	5	11	2	8	6
Fruity Floating Islands (p. 81)	151	5	23	4	63	281	8	30	11	3	12	5	8	5
Lime Mousse (p. 74)	179	5	20	9	31	49	7	7	5	2	5	0	2	3
Orange-Strawberry Sponge Cake (p. 77)	265	5	51	5	93	148	8	7	47	8	10	5	3	8
Pineapple-Coconut Cream Puffs (p. 74)	142	4	17	6	103	80	6	8	4	7	7	3	2	5
Pineapple Frost (p. 85)	385	2	40	25	30	210	4	22	16	6	7	1	8	2
Pinwheel Pears with Raspberry Sauce (p. 89)	178	4	24	9	51	232	6	7	20	4	8	2	5	4
Raspberry Soufflé (p. 75)	98	4	19	1	45	112	5	4	19	2	7	2	5	3
Rhubarb-Banana Bread Pudding (p. 78)	107	145	4	28	90	245	6	17	9	6	7	4	5	6
Strawberry-Rice Fluff (p. 79)	301	7	39	14	67	286	10	12	83	7	15	5	12	7

Index

Index

TIPS